LOVE MY COUNTRY,
Loathe My Government

Fifty First Steps to Restoring Our
Freedom and Destroying the
American Political Class

Walter "Bruno" Korschek

Love My Country, Loathe My Government

Published by Wheatmark®
610 East Delano Street, Suite 104
Tucson, Arizona 85705 U.S.A.
www.wheatmark.com

International Standard Book Number: 978-1-60494-278-1
Library of Congress Control Number: 2009925415

Speical thanks to my wife and son, Cheryl and Michael, for their support and input. And also to the ignorance, arrogance, and misdeeds of the political class for making this book possible.

Table of Contents

ENERGY INDEPENDENCE

SOCIAL ISSUES

FOREIGN POLICY

POLITICAL BEHAVIOR

CORPORATE GOVERNANCE

WHAT YOU CAN DO

APPENDICES

Acknowledgments—Part 1

Most of the ideas and concepts in this book are not new. While this may be the first time they have been presented in such a manner, the issue of freedom, country, and the intrusion of government has been written about and analyzed by many intelligent and articulate people. I would like to acknowledge four authors who had the most influence in the development of this book and resultant action plan:

Restoring the American Dream by Robert Ringer, copyright 1979, published by QED and distributed by Harper & Row. While this book was first published in 1979, its relevance today has not slipped at all. Mr. Ringer does a fantastic job of stripping away the myths of government that the political class uses to chip away the freedoms that the Constitution sets forth. He explodes favorite government catchphrases such as the "voluntary tax systems" (it is not voluntary), the "good of society" (as defined by the political class), etc. It is a straightforward, powerful work that everyone should read in order to understand how the political class manipulates you and the country, and in the process reduces your individual freedom. He also does an excellent job showing how the political class astutely turns one group of citizens against another ("special interest groups"), not to improve the country but to get itself elected.

The Government Racket 2000: All New Washington Waste from A to Z by Martin L. Gross, copyright 2000, published by Avon Books. Written eight years ago, it could be easily written today (by just updating and increasing the number of tax dollars spent on wasteful government programs). There are far too many misspending instances from the book to list here but consider the following examples:

- $5.6 million spent to fix the scoreboard for the Anaheim Angels (a major league baseball team and a privately owned and operated company) after an earthquake.

- $5.0 million spent to build a new parliament building in the Solomon Islands, a part of the British Commonwealth.

- $1.5 million federal study of parking at truck stops.

- Over $200,000 for a cat and dog census in a California county.

If these and other programs were not so expensive they would be laughable. Unfortunately, the misuse of tax dollars on these parochial programs reduces every taxpayer's economic freedom.

Why Government Does Not Work by Harry Brown, copyright 1995, published by Martin's Press. A scholarly work that goes into the reasons why government and its actions almost always result in wasted resources/tax dollars, non-accomplishment of the stated goals, and a reduction in individual freedom.

Free to Choose by Milton Friedman, published by Harcourt Brace Jovanovich. Mr. Friedman was one of the most accomplished economic minds of our time. His insights into the continuous failings of government policies, as perpetrated by the political class, is enlightening.

I apologize to other sources for putting forth ideas of theirs that were not from the above list. It was not my intention to say they were my own; it is only that they were so good, they had to be included in this book.

Acknowledgements—Part 2

Although most of this book is highly critical of the current set of sitting politicians and the whole political class, these criticisms are in no way meant to denigrate or call into question the hard work put forth every day by the employees that work for all levels of government. In talking with friends and relatives who currently work in government, I sense that they have the same feelings of frustration with the current state of politics in this country. In fact, many of them are probably more frustrated than others since they see firsthand how much waste and how many poor decisions the political class creates every day.

In any human endeavor, whether it is in the corporate, athletic, or governmental world, leadership is the key to success. Having talented and hardworking employees or teammates is great, but it takes strong and intelligent leadership to integrate that effort and talent to be successful. Thus, while most government employees are working just as hard as those in the private sector, the lack of leadership by the political class is wasting their talents, insights, and energy. Their efforts and dedication are appreciated, and they should not be held in the same low esteem that the country currently holds for the political class.

Introduction

When work began on this book, it was the summer of 2007 and everything should have been good in the United States. Unemployment had been at historic lows for a number of years. The stock market had steadily risen for over five years. There had not been another domestic terrorist attack since September 11, 2001. The United States was still the economic, military, and cultural superpower in the world. More people than ever owned their own home and their own business. New technology continued to make work and play more efficient and fulfilling. It was the summer of 2007 and everything should have been good in America.

But it was not good, and it still isn't. There is a nagging doubt in the country that all is not well under the surface. While most everyone has a job, it seems that only the very top of the employment hierarchy is making true economic progress, many times by breaking both the law and accounting standards. While people are employed, they cannot save anything as energy prices and other prices continue to rise, while the burden of taxation at all government levels continues to crush economic freedom. Politicians do not solve problems, they only get elected. Government programs and institutions usually do not work and in many cases make bad conditions worse. We are bogged down in a war in Iraq that was ill conceived, ill run, and ill planned. Political scandals, sex and otherwise, and outright lawbreaking by politicians seems to be a constant. Home mortgage defaults and foreclosures are at an all-time high as more and more people lose their homes to rising interest rates, shady mortgage dealings, and lax government oversight. Toys and other products from overseas are sometimes dangerous or fatal. All is not good in the United States.

However, I would contend that the United States as a country is still fine. It has the most generous, hardworking, creative people in the world by most measures. They are forgiving and trusting and, for the most part, accepting of others. And they still are probably the most individually free people anywhere. The root cause of many of our problems is not the United States the country but the United States the government, two different entities. In theory, the government of a free country should reflect and protect the ideals and dreams of *all* of the people in that country. It should not control the country, it should protect the country and its ideals in the most minimalist way possible.

Make no mistake, there is a significant difference between the country and the government of that country. Recall the famous words of John Kennedy when he said:

> Ask not what your country can do for you—ask what you can do for your country.

Now, take that quote and tweak it just a bit:

> Ask not what your government can do for you—ask what you can do for your government.

Most politicians from America's political class would see no difference between these two statements. They do not understand they should be serving the country as they run the government, not serving the government (i.e., themselves), as they run the country.

While America may have two political parties, it now has only one political class. Its main purpose is to get its members elected and control the government; it is not to get elected and serve the country. They generally view elected office as a lifelong perk and a career, and not as a patriotic calling. In the process, individual rights are trampled, individual financial freedom is taxed out of existence, economic progress is stunted, young Americans are maimed and killed, and the country and its freedoms suffer horribly.

Let's be very clear: as a country and as individual citizens we are not as free as we should be, as we were, or as we think we are. The reduction in this country's freedom is a direct result of the increased power of the American political class. And this swing in power has not been to the betterment of any of us outside of that political class. Freedom is what made this country great. The Clintons, the Bushes, the Kennedys, and their kind did not, and will never be the reasons why America is great.

The purpose of this book is to illuminate some of the myths of government and the political class and set forth a relatively simple and straightforward fifty first steps to restore America's heritage and freedoms. These are not earth shattering steps and ideas. In fact, they are quite easy to understand and agree on. However, the fact that the current political class has not moved on any of these steps illustrates either a lack of courage, a lack of intelligence, or a selfishness to maintain the status quo, protect their interests, and not enhance the country.

Sometimes I wonder whether the world is being run by smart people who are putting us on, or imbeciles who really mean it.

—Mark Twain

Who Should Not Read this Book

The following people should not read this book:

Those who are convinced that politicians know what is best for us. Have you ever met a politician? Most of us have not, so how would a politician possibly know what is best for you and me? Each American citizen comes from a unique background of economic strata, religion, home life, life experiences, health, etc. No politician who talks about the "common good" or what is best for "us" is trying to preserve our freedom; they are trying to impose their concept of how we should behave. The promise of America was that the country recognized each person as an individual and provided the means for each individual to succeed or fail according to their own abilities and effort. How refreshing would it be for a politician to believe that his or her job was to maximize our freedom and ability and not determine what the "common good" should be.

Those who are convinced that politicians are smarter than us because they got elected. Getting elected, particularly lately, is not a function of brains, but a function of money and public relations specialists. Ronald Reagan once said that "The best minds are not in government. If any were, business would steal them away." Examples abound of stupid politicians. Whether it is getting caught having an affair with an intern while a massive investigation of his life was underway, soliciting sex in an airport men's room, courting underage Congressional pages, etc., the ability of politicians to do and say stupid things should never be underestimated.

Unfortunately, their actions and stupidity come at the expense of our tax dollars and freedom.

Republicans who think the country would be better off if the Democrats would just go away. In the early 2000s, the Republicans controlled the presidency, the House of Representatives, and the Senate. As a result of this control, they were able to accomplish virtually nothing of importance, continuing to waste taxpayer dollars and persecuting homosexuals and abortion supporters while other, larger issues (failing public education, continuing drug addiction problems, rising energy dependence on foreign energy sources, etc.) went unattended. They initiated an ill-conceived invasion of Iraq and got involved with high-powered lobbyists such as Jack Abramoff in kickback after kickback scheme.

Democrats who think the country would be better off if the Republicans would just go away. The Democrats are no better. Most of the large corporate accounting scandals (Enron, Worldcom, Aegis, Qwest) were perpetrated while a Democrat was in the White House and his SEC was unable to uncover the massive fraud that bankrupted the retirement and investment dreams of thousands of American families. It was the Republican administration that brought these corporate lawbreakers to justice. It was during a Democrat administration when America first came under terrorist attacks (first World Trade Center bombing, *USS Cole*, African embassy bombings) and did nothing to effectively counteract the growing threat of Islamic terrorism. It was a Democrat administration that allowed numerous anticompetition mergers in the energy arena (e.g., Exxon-Mobil) to become a reality, contributing to the current energy crisis.

The bottom line is that over the past thirty years, both political parties (but the same political class) have had the chance to make the American government better at serving and protecting the country, its citizens, and the freedoms guaranteed by the Constitution. The political class has failed miserably at every turn. The reality is that the Democrats need the Republicans and vice versa. In order to stay in power they each need an enemy to energize their base—that is, they need to destroy the freedoms of certain citizens to gain the votes of others.

Those who think that a two-party political system works best. Nowhere in the Constitution does it call for only two political parties. Many other countries have more than two substantive parties and they seem to work fine. Why should we have to settle for only two, and why only these two? Their track record is horrific and they have not protected our freedoms over time. And remember, while there may be two political parties, there is only one political class, generally populated by rather unintelligent, unimaginative, and uncourageous people whose ambition is to get elected and stay elected by whatever means possible.

Those who believe that if you do not vote you get the government you deserve. By not voting, many people are actually voicing their opinion. I believe that many Americans fail to vote not because they are apathetic, but because the political class has rigged the system so that the resultant choices for office are so unattractive that it is not worth the effort to go out and vote. Under their reasoning, the lesser of two evils, Republican versus Democrat, is still evil. In the Soviet Union, everyone was required to vote, and they got the governments they deserved, governments that included some of the most oppressive, cutthroat, freedom-hating regimes of all time, from Stalin on forward. By rigging the system through the control of the primary schedule, control of the money sources, gerrymandering Congressional districts, control of government regulations, etc., we never get a true choice at the voting booth. Evil is evil whether Republican or a Democrat.

> **An election cannot give a country a firm sense of direction if it has two or more national parties which merely have different names but are as alike in their principles and aims as two peas in a pod.**
>
> —*Franklin Delano Roosevelt*

Reference Vignettes

As you read through the fifty ways to destroy the ruling American political class and restore American freedoms, keep the following vignettes and images in your mind. Hopefully, they will demystify what government is and strip away the fallacies of government that the political class wants you to believe:

JABBA THE HUTT = AMERICAN POLITICAL CLASS = U.S. GOVERNMENT

What is government? Most people have not spent the time to try and figure out what government actually is. Most consider some type of omnipotent entity with varying degrees of use and brains. The clichés of 1) "The government will pay for it" and 2) "I'm from the government and I am here to help you" are commonly used as surrogates for what government is. Unfortunately, government does not pay for anything (you do through taxation), and when was the last time any major government program ever cost-efficiently helped you?

Government is really nothing more than the political class parading as Jabba the Hutt from Star Wars. As you may recall, Jabba was a formless, overweight entity that ruled with an iron fist while devouring resources brought to him. He did not pay for anything (he took it) and he was not there to help anyone but himself. Those he ruled over had no say in how their resources were spent and had no chance in dislodging him from power. Sound familiar? Substitute politicians for the Jabba the Hutt and you pretty much get a definition of what government is in America today.

Remember, while Jabba runs the American government, America the country is basically still fine. Americans are good people represented by bad politicians that would make Jabba proud.

THE BENEVOLENT MOBSTER

The benevolent mobster is a mobster who breaks your kneecaps but gets you a discount on the cost of crutches. While you are thankful for the discount, you would not have needed the crutches in the first place if the mobster had not broken your kneecaps. Government works the same way as the benevolent mobster. Most government programs and laws are a result of a previous government action that went awry or never worked to begin with. With each additional government action, the situation is generally not fixed, but just becomes screwed up in a different way.

One example of this phenomenon is the economic stimulus package that the political class passed in the spring of 2008. To help revive the consumer side of the economy, taxpayers received a check worth up to $1,200 by late summer of 2008 in hopes that they would spend the money and stimulate the economy. While we were happy to be receiving a check, would it not have been easier to not tax us so much to begin with? In that case we could have had the money already. The checks we received was our money to begin with!

Another example of the benevolent mobster is the property tax rebate program in New Jersey. Every year New Jersey property taxpayers eagerly await their property tax rebate check from the state government, acting as if they are getting something for free. However, while they are happy to get a check, wouldn't it be easier not to tax property owners as much to begin with and let them keep their money initially?

THE FROG IN THE BEAKER

If you boil water in a beaker and put a frog in it, he will immediately sense the danger and try to change the situation of danger to one of safety. However, if you place the frog in a beaker with room temperature water, he is pretty happy and comfortable. If you gradually increase the temperature he is initially still happy (kind of feels like a spa treatment!), but he does not notice the increasing danger since the change in temperature is too subtle. Before he realizes he needs to get out it is too late.

Government programs as perpetuated by the political class work the same way. They usually start out with a high purpose and much fanfare, and while they may reduce freedoms a little bit, it is a small price to pay for the programs' benefits (which are never delivered). Many Americans have that funny feeling today that while life seems okay on the surface, it is getting a little warm in here. The heat is getting dangerously high as the political class exerts more and more power over the country and its citizens, destroying both in the process.

THE FREEDOM PYRAMID

The basis of America is the Constitution, which laid out how government would be structured. This structure would help fulfill the promise of the Constitution and the rights and freedoms it laid out for the country and its citizens. This document and its implementation allowed America to become the freest and most prosperous country in the history of the world. It placed individual freedom above all else, including government and politicians, who existed to protect the rights and freedoms of the individual. One way to illustrate and understand the intended relationships between individuals, freedoms, government, and the Constitution is with a pyramid:

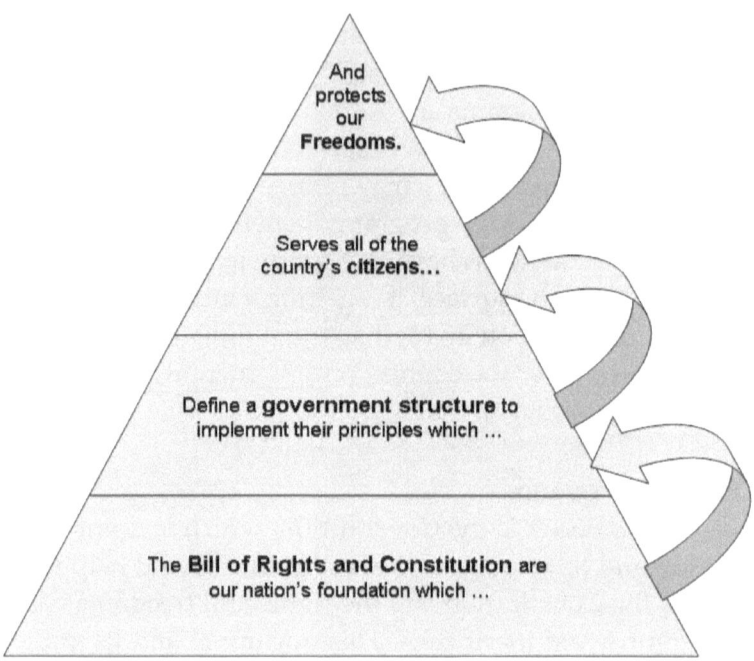

However, over time, the political class changed this relationship in order to increase their power at the expense of the country's. They were not content to be the unglamorous foundation which supported freedom, they wanted the glory of being higher up on the pyramid:

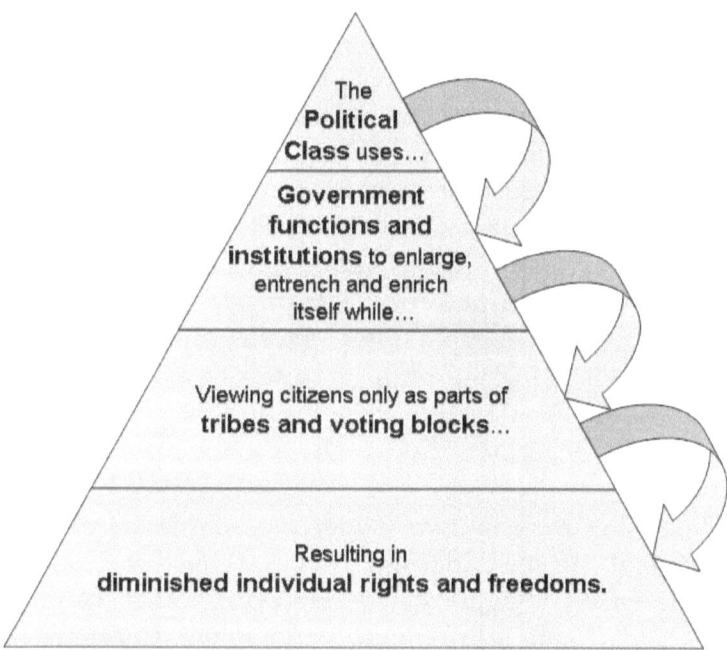

Obviously, there are a number of significant changes in how the political class views freedom. Your individual freedom is now at the bottom of the pyramid. Your only function to the political class is to be grouped into favorable tribes or "special interest groups" (e.g., gay Americans, African Americans, Christian Americans, Jewish Americans, Native Americans, soccer moms, NASCAR dads, etc.).

Once grouped into these broader categories, the government can then be used by the political class to get themselves elected and dictate how you should behave. I have removed the Constitution and country from the second pyramid since they no longer serve those at the top of the pyramid. The political class uses them or ignores them to serve their purposes.

For America to survive and thrive again, we must revert back to the first pyramid of power and freedom.

GEORGE ORWELL'S *1984*—OCEANIA VERSUS EURASIA VERSUS EASTASIA

In 1949, George Orwell wrote the novel *1984*, a fictional account of how humanity's freedom would be stripped away in the future and controlled by a single elitist ruling political group. In his book, the world is separated into three super states: Oceania, Eurasia and Eastasia. These three super states are in a constant state of conflict which one would assume is a bad thing. However, the ruling political classes in each state see it as a good thing. The constant conflicts allow them to stay in power by focusing their citizens' attention and wrath on the other super states, ignoring the fact that their own political class is using the conflicts to stay in power. It is in their best interest to keep the conflicts going and focus attention on the "enemies," not their own shortcomings or the resulting decline in freedom.

While there are only two "super states," the Republicans and the Democrats, in the nation today, they behave in a very similar manner to Orwell's "super states." However, rather than directing the hate and attention to faraway nations, the American political class keeps up an active conflict between the supporters of the two political parties or "super states." The two political parties within the single political class pick their friends (special interest groups) and pick their enemies in order to get their friends excited about reelecting the same tired politicians over and over again. By pitting citizen against citizen, the political class is able to continue to get elected without having to make any serious or courageous decisions to help freedom or benefit the country. The endgame is to get elected regardless of who you make the enemy out to be: "Elect me or *those people* might take control." Or, according to an Orwell quote: "The primary aim of modern warfare is to use up the products of the machine without raising the general standard of living." In other words, by working up our own special interest groups and pitting them against their special interests group, we can divert attention from the real problems and use the conflict to stay in power.

This Orwellian strategy is a very dangerous road for freedom. America was always known as the melting pot where different people from different nationalities, different races, different religions, different lifestyles, etc., could eventually integrate into America and could live free, private, and prosperous lives. We did not have the hardcore "tribal" problems that exist for most people throughout the world, be they Croats, Serbs, and Muslims in Yugoslavia, Hutus and Tutsis in Africa, or Shiites, Sunnis, and Kurds in Iraq. History has shown the disastrous consequences of dividing a nation into distinct tribes, the exact strategy the American political class is pursuing today.

Take this quiz. What do the following people have in common:

- Gay Americans
- African Americans
- Hispanic Americans
- Christian Americans
- White Americans
- Jewish Americans
- Agnostic Americans
- Elderly Americans
- Gen X Americans
- Gen Y Americans
- Homeless Americans
- Elected Americans
- Southern/Northern/Eastern/Western Americans
- Rich Americans
- Poor Americans
- Blue State Americans
- Red State Americans

Obviously, they are all Americans. While the adjective in front of "Americans" helps to describe their culture and their individual beliefs and lifestyles, the adjectives should never be used to suppress the rights of other adjectives. A white U.S. senator in DC should have the exact same rights as the older gay Hispanic Jewish homeless person in North Dakota. Only when we recognize and respect individual differences will every American be freer, and the tribes trend will be reversed.

THE FIVE-LEGGED DOG

Riddle (believed to have come from Abraham Lincoln): If you called a tail a leg, how many legs would a dog have?

Answer: Four. Just because you called a tail a leg does not mean it is a leg.

Consider the following short passage from Orwell's *1984*:

"War is peace, freedom is slavery, ignorance is strength."

The political class are masters at the old saying that if you cannot dazzle them with brilliance than baffle them with BS. The political class does not want you, the American citizen, to understand all that it does because if you did, you would realize what a wasteful and dangerous path they have put this country on. Better to come up with a catchy slogan in order to baffle them than to dazzle them. Consider just a handful of examples:

- The Patriot Act sounds great, as if it is going to resurrect the freedoms and liberties that used to be available in this country. Unfortunately, as is the case with most political class slogans, it describes just the opposite. The Patriot Act greatly reduces individual freedoms and liberties, providing more and more ways for the political class to assert its control.

- Reagan's 1980s "Peacemaker" nuclear weapons program. Regardless of whether it was needed, did anyone really think that increasing the number of deployed nuclear weapons was helping to keep the peace?

- The Social Security Trust Fund is a classic five-legged-dog program. Yourdictionary.com defines "trust fund" as "money, securities, etc. held in trust." Unfortunately, Social Security does not conform to this definition. It "holds" nothing, it immediately takes the input from citizens who pay into the system and gives it to retirees, spending the overpayment on regular, non-Social Security political class programs. If you "trust" and believe that the government is holding onto the money you pay into the Social Security System, you are falling for this five-legged-dog program.

Snappy slogans should never be a substitute for serving the country and its citizens or solving real national problems. Unfortunately, most of the time the political class is too selfish, unable, or unwilling to come up with anything better.

BARBECUE MITTENS VERSUS SURGICAL GLOVES

Imagine they are wheeling you into the operating room for major surgery and you notice your doctor has on big, clumsy barbeque mittens rather than tight, flexible latex gloves. Imagine your fear when he tells you that he will execute the operation wearing the barbecue mittens. The political class, through their government programs and laws, usually work the same way. Even when they have a worthwhile, thought-through plan, the political class execution of it is usually clumsy, inefficient, and wasteful. There is never any elegance to their thinking or implementation. As a result, your tax dollars and the freedom they could result in are grossly wasted.

In the 1990s there was a lot of activity to save the American farmer. Farm Aid concerts raised funds for the effort and Congress eventually passed a massive farm aid bill. While the bill may have saved many family farms, it also enriched the large food processing and corporate farm businesses who were not in need of saving. A simple solution may have been to cap the aid to only family-owned farms (excluding the conglomerates) or basing the aid on need, using latex gloves instead of clumsy and inefficient barbecue mitts.

As another example, the current Social Security program will go bankrupt in the next several decades. Rather than cap payouts today for those Americans who clearly do not need the money (Bill Gates, Donald Trump, etc.) in order to help those who do, the cur-

rent system the political class has in place sees no distinction between need and want. Why operate efficiently with latex gloves
when barbecue mitts can still do the job?

Economic Freedom = Political Freedom

Probably the most profound observation in Ringer's *Restoring
the American Dream* is that a citizen cannot have true freedom in
America if he or she does not have economic or financial freedom.
According to the 2007 estimates from the Tax Foundation, the political class in America today demands that, on average, almost four
months of work be done by an American worker in order to pay for
the upkeep of government and the ruling political class. In other
words, the average American works almost to May 1 for the government each year. Only at that point does the average American
worker start working for themselves and their family.

We spend so much time and effort paying taxes that our options
for lifestyle and personal choices are severely limited. Imagine that
you were able to keep all of the money and wealth you made. What
would you do? Maybe you or your spouse would decide to stay at
home and not work a second job in order to spend more quality
time with your kids. Maybe you would take the additional money
and donate it to charitable causes. Maybe you would start up your
own business. Maybe you would save it for your children to get a
better education.

And the situation at all levels of government is getting worse.
More and more it seems that the function of government and the
ruling class is to see how much more deviously they can separate
you from your earnings in order to feed the inefficient government
beast. From spreading legalized gambling to increasing sin taxes
(alcohol and cigarette taxes) to new innovative programs/fees/li-
censing, government is addicted to our wealth and the addiction is
growing at the expense of our freedom.

Without taxation, your freedom of choice would expand expo-
nentially. However, the political class does not want that or they
would not tax you so much. They want to decide what to do with
your hard-earned money for the "common good," reducing your
choices and life options in the process. Remember, the government

does not pay for anything. It funds everything it does by forcibly taking your wealth for its purposes.

"LET THEM EAT CAKE" SYNDROME

Still not convinced there is a distinct political class in this country that thinks they come first and that we should settle for what they deem appropriate for us? Consider the following:

- While working Americans continue to find fewer and fewer companies offering traditional pensions, and only 50 percent of American employees can participate in a 401(k) retirement program (*Parade Magazine*, April 27, 2008), members of the political class not only get very rich pensions after retirement, but they also partake in the Social Security system benefits and a government 401(k)-like retirement savings plan. In addition, their robust traditional, taxpayer-funded monthly pension is adjusted upward every year, unlike many other American pensions that are set at a fixed level at retirement with no future increase possible.

- While you and your company struggle to get health care spending under control with individuals paying more and more each year for less and less, the political class continues to get world-class medical care, much better than anything else you and I can get.

- Several years ago when their was a severe flu shot vaccine shortage at the onset of flu season, we were told to make sure that only the sickly, the old, and the young would be able to get flu shots. However, at the same time that this directive was coming out of Washington, the political class was shown on TV getting inoculated regardless of their age or health.

- Although all other Washington DC citizens pay Washington DC income taxes, federal politicians and two of their top staffers are exempt from paying these taxes along with not having to pay Washington DC sales taxes for anything purchased in the Capitol Building.

- They and all members of their staff get free long-distance phone service at both their offices and their homes.

The political class give themselves all of these perks even though over a hundred of them in Congress are self-declared millionaires.

Useless Used Car Lemon versus Useless Government Efforts

Imagine you bought a used car (or any product or service for that matter), and within weeks of the purchase the tires went flat, the wipers scratched the windshield, the transmission locked up, the radio went silent, and the cost of operating this car was far more than promised. I would bet that most of us would immediately return the defective purchase to the seller and demand a refund, repairs, or other remedies. Why Americans do not behave this way in response to the political class is a vexing paradox because when you think about it, the government programs that are run by and authorized by the political class, but paid for by you and I, work just as poorly as that lemon of a car:

- *Social Security.* Going broke.

- *Medicare.* Going broke

- *FEMA.* Ask the people in New Orleans

- *Border Patrol.* There are over twelve million illegal aliens already in the country and no effective plans or strategy in place to prevent more.

- *National Energy Program and Strategy.* Virtually nonexistent.

- *Campaign finance reform laws.* Probably unconstitutional and not effective anyway.

- *NASA.* Dangerous, life-threatening shuttle program and a space station program that under performs but goes over budget.

- *Federal Trade Commission.* Tainted food and toys continue to flood into the country from overseas, posing serious health threats to Americans.

- *Federal tax system.* Overly complicated, overly expensive, and leaking like a sieve from non-payers.

- *Highway system.* A bridge collapse in Minnesota and the falling concrete panels in Boston's Big Dig illustrate the fatal ramifications of the government's highway programs.

And why do government functions no longer work? Maybe what the political class has been focusing on lately has something to do with it:

- A Congressional hearing and government resources were deployed to see if a single over-the-hill major league baseball pitcher took steroids nine years ago. Why bother with Iraq—is Roger Clemens juicing?

- A U.S. senator wanted to know if an NFL football team broke league rules by videotaping an opposing team's hand signals in a football game six years ago. Why bother with the health-care crisis—are the Patriots' Super Bowl championship titles tainted by cheating?

- As a result of House speaker Nancy Pelosi's "Greening the Capitol" campaign, the House cafeteria now serves hamburgers made from "humanely raised, antibiotic beef," Fair Trade and shade-grown coffee, "cage free" chicken, and rBGH free milk (*LA Times* as reported in *The Week,* February 22, 2008). Why bother with U.S. kids sucking on lead-tainted imported toys—are Congressional people eating healthy?

Nothing works in this country, just like nothing works in the junker of a car, and Americans know who is to blame. In late February, 2008, President Bush had an approval rating of 30 percent and Congress had an approval rating of only 22 percent (*AP-Ipsos,* as reported in *The Week,* February 22, 2008). Think about recent national problems and when the political class took action:

- *9-ll attacks.* It was not until several years later when the 9-11 Commission Report came out with an analysis of what went wrong. Several years after the attack.

- *Tainted products from China.* - Political class stirs only after people start getting sick from tainted imports.

- *Hurricane Katrina.* Political class expresses outrage after New Orleans is devastated. Several years later New Orleans is still a mess.

- *Subprime mortgage crisis.* Political class expresses concern after banks and homeowners start to default as a result of shoddy mortgage practices and lax government oversight.

- *Gasoline prices.* Political class is outraged after gasoline prices hit an all-time high despite knowing for over thirty years an energy crisis was looming.

- *Substandard military hospital facilities.* Political class is outraged after wounded soldiers return stateside to horrendous medical facilities.

Its only *after* a crisis that the political class wakes up and starts posturing (but hardly ever doing anything effective) even though the problem has smacked them in the face. Rarely are they proactive in preventing a crisis. It's time to dump this lemon of a used car and the political class that got us in this mess. *Turn the page for the first fifty steps.*

Politics is the art of looking for trouble, finding it everywhere, diagnosing it incorrectly, and applying the wrong remedies.

—Groucho Marx

Taxes

Step 1

Establish a five-year program that reduces the size
of the federal government budget and expenditures
by 10 percent a year in all departments.

As stated in the introduction, American taxpayers have paid more and more of their hard-earned wealth to all levels of government over the years while receiving less and less government benefit in return. Consider just some of the different types of taxes that many of us pay during the course of our lives:

Federal income tax
State income tax
City income tax
Sales tax—State
Sales tax—county
Property tax
Social Security tax
Medicare tax
Gasoline tax
Capital gains tax
Telephone taxes
Hotel tax
Rental car tax
Airport taxes
Estate tax

Unemployment tax

Gift tax

Luxury taxes

These are eighteen of the bigger taxes, but I am sure there are many others in different parts of the country. And this list does not include "licenses" and "fees," which are just other words for tax. According to the Tax Foundation, Americans send a third of their wealth every year to the government, theoretically working for the government/political class until late April.

And remember, there is a direct link between financial freedom and true freedom. By sucking taxpayers of nearly 33 percent of their income, the political class severely limits your freedom to run your life as you please. With such a high tax level, your ability to start a business, save for your kids' education, save for the retirement you want, help others in need, or stay home and help raise your kids is virtually extinguished by the government and the political class.

And what do we get for this large chunk of our wealth? Not very much. Just look at the government/political class's incompetence list in the introduction. Nothing works anymore, whether it is FEMA's impotent reaction to Hurricane Katrina, a Social Security system heading to insolvency, an aging space shuttle fleet that has been fatal more than once, etc., etc., etc.

Given the situation, it is time to take back our economic freedom and the political/personal freedom that goes with it. Thus, the most important step of all fifty steps is to begin downsizing the beast known as the government. All human endeavors tend to expand to the time and resources allocated to fulfill that endeavor. When American corporations went through the downsizing trauma of the 1980s and 1990s, they realized that they had indeed many areas of excess expense that could be cut without sacrificing profits and customer service. There is no reason to believe that the federal government, which has *never* had a good housecleaning, cannot reduce its size significantly without sacrificing service.

This change would occur over a five-year period, with every department in the federal government reducing its expenditures by 10 percent a year. This would be done through a zero-based approach. That is, if you were starting the government today, what programs, departments, expenditures, assets, etc., would truly be needed and essential to provide a viable government service to a large number of Americans?

This annual 10 percent reduction could be attained by any number of different strategies:

- The easiest way is to reduce the size of the federal payroll. By using a zero-based budgeting approach, reducing programs should result in a reduction in headcount. According to a March 10, 2008, article in *Newsweek*, about 50 percent of the current federal employee base will retire by 2012. This situation provides a unique opportunity to pare government's size by attrition, by severely limiting the number of people hired to replace retiring federal employees.

- However, as the downsizing corporations realized, you can only cut headcount so much; it is the expense and cost of operations where many cost savings can be found. And who best to find those efficiencies but those Federal employees who work the problem every day? To make use of their expertise, a Web-based process could be set up for suggestions on how to trim expenses and costs from those who really know what is going on, and not the elected official who just arrived on the scene. (Anyone who watched the 2005 and 2008 Congressional hearings on the use of steroids by professional baseball players quickly realized that members of the political class are not the sharpest knives in the drawer when it comes to getting at the root cause of a problem.)

- The motivation of government employees for helping to downsize will be twofold: 1) Identifying excess costs in the operations means a smaller chance that the 10 percent reduction will come from headcount reductions. 2) Employees who make suggestions that make a difference will be eligible on a lottery basis for a cut of the savings. For example, if someone suggests an operations improvement that led to a $1 million savings, they will be entered into a random drawing pool with a chance to get 5 percent of the savings as a reward.

- Another relatively easy way to find the savings is to abide by a new pork barrel principle: any federal program that does not significantly impact the citizens in at least five states will be terminated. If the program is still needed, then the citizens in the affected states will pay for them themselves; the federal government will not. Efforts like the "bridge to nowhere" in Alaska will never again be a federal issue. If New York senators Clinton and Shuman want to build a $1 million tribute to the Woodstock music festival in Woodstock, New York, let them do it with New York state taxpayer money. There are tens of billions of dollars that can be returned to taxpayers every year if something like this minimum five-state program is implemented.

- There are many other innovative (another characteristic one would not usually attribute to a member of the political class) ways to save money that are more subtle. For example, Harvard University has an endowment of over $30 billion. They earn tax-free investment income on that endowment every year. Let's do some simple math:

  Let's say they invest the entire $30 billion in Treasury bills and high-grade bonds, easily earning 4 percent return annually. That approach will generate $1.2 billion a year.

  There are about eight thousand kids at Harvard who will pay about $50 thousand a year for room, board, and tuition if there is no financial aid. Their total expenditure then will be $400 million a year.

Thus, using a very conservative investment approach, Harvard can pay the *entire bill for its entire student body every year, never touch its principle*, and still have almost *$800 million* left over every year.

Given its wealth, it makes no sense for any student going to Harvard, or to any other wealthy university, to have their education subsidized by the American taxpayer. Thus, no student going to Harvard or other wealthy, tax-free investing university would be eligible for federal student financial aid. The federal student program would immediately be down-sized by forcing the wealthy, tax-free investing private universities in the country to put up their own wealth to get the students they desire.

- One of the biggest budget items is the total cost of the military. There are two major budget cut areas, one short-term and one long-term, available in this area. Short-term, we should immediately shut down and bring home any troops overseas that serve no vital security need. The two biggest withdrawls would be in South Korea and Japan. Depending on the measurement methodology, South Korea has about the twelfth biggest economy in the world, and they require all citizens to serve two years in the armed forces (i.e., they have enough armed forces to guard the border). Thus, they can afford to pay for their own defense. Removing thirty thousand Korean-based U.S. troops would possibly have a secondary political effect of reducing tensions on the Korean peninsula in addition to shrinking military expenditures.

And why we have any troops in Japan is a mystery to me. Japan is unlikely to take up arms again for Pearl Harbor II, and saying their deployment is necessary to deter China is a ridiculous statement. Stationing twenty-five thousand U.S. troops halfway around the world in Japan while China has an army in excess of two million soldiers (New York Times Online, March 5, 2008) is not going to deter anyone. Bring them home and save the money.

The longer-term opportunity is to not get so involved in the rest of the world's problems. This would eventually result a smaller U.S. military and less resentment directed toward us from the rest of the world. This does not mean that we would immediately get out of Afghanistan and Iraq. These efforts have to be seen to a successful, long-term end. However, hopefully in the future we would not be so hasty and anxious to get involved in the first place.

Who would holler at this budget-cutting exercise? First and foremost would be members of the political class. Less budget means less power, and power is what they crave. The military would also be smaller, meaning less power for those in command. And of course, those entities that live off the pork of Washington (e.g., defense contractors) would also lose funding and power. However, the increase in their power has come at the expense of your economic freedom.

The core problem is not that the "rich" do not pay enough in taxes. According to a April 14, 2008, *Fortune* magazine article:

> In 2005 (the last year data is available), the bottom 40 percent of Americans by income had, in aggregate, an effective tax rate that's negative. Their households received more money through the income tax system, largely through the earned income tax credit, than they paid … The top 10 percent of taxpayers kicked in 70 percent of the total income tax. And the famous 1 percent paid 40 percent of all income tax, a proportion that has jumped dramatically since 1986.

The core problem is that the political class spends too much, not that the rich do not pay enough. Don't allow the political class to play the tribes (rich versus poor) against each other. Once they can divert attention from them spending too much, the cause is lost and taxpayer wealth will not be returned to the taxpayers.

Like the frog in the beaker, it's starting to get very warm in this country as the political class turns up the heat to get its hands on as much of your wealth as possible rather than turning down the heat by downsizing the government it runs.

I'm proud to be paying taxes in the United States. The only thing is—I could be just as proud for half the money.

—Arthur Godfrey

Step 2

Use the first annual 10 percent reduction to offset
the federal deficit.

If you really want to start worrying about the future of this country, I suggest you read up on the position of David M. Walker, Comptroller General of the United States. Consider some excerpts from an article he wrote for his hometown paper, *The Birmingham* (Alabama) *News* on January 20, 2008:

- The nation's financial condition is worse than advertised.

- We face large and growing structural deficits in future years, due primarily to the impending retirement of the baby boom generation.

- The nation's unfunded commitments for Social Security and Medicare alone have risen to $53 trillion in the past seven years. That's *trillion* with twelve trailing zeroes. These unfunded commitments are rising $2 to 3 trillion (that's *trillion* with 12 trailing zeroes) every year.

- $53 trillion comes out to about $175 thousand of debt load for every American, including newborn infants, or about $455 thousand for every American household.

This country is hurtling toward an economic meltdown that the political class is unwilling or unable to slow down. The numbers above are not from some doomsday crackpot. They are from a seriously trained, accounting professional who sees firsthand how bad this country's financial status is. It is possible that the downfall of this country will not be because of the Civil War, Adolph Hitler, Benito Mussolini, Tojo, communism, Joseph Stalin, OPEC, or Osama Bin Laden, but because the political class bankrupted the country.

Consider another view of this country's mounting debt. According to a July 23, 2007, article at www.business.timeonline. co.uk, Japan owns $623 billion in U.S. Treasury bonds, China owns $397 billion in U.S. Treasury bonds, and oil exporters own $110 billion in U.S. Treasury bonds. Thus, at least $1 trillion (that's *trillion* with twelve trailing zeroes) that the United States owes to people and governments we have no control over. Lack of control goes hand in hand with lack of freedom.

Therefore, the first 10 percent of savings will be used to start paying down the enormous amount of debt the political class has rung up through the years. No less than the survival of the country is at risk. This 10 percent would be set aside every year to pay down the national debt.

Like Jabba the Hutt, government and the political class consumes more and more, bloating itself beyond recognition and effectiveness. And like Jabba's fate, the end will not be pretty unless something is done soon.

The genius of our ruling class is that it has kept a majority of the people from ever questioning the inequity of a system where most people drudge along, paying heavy taxes for which they get nothing in return.

—Gore Vidal

Step 3

Use the second annual 10 percent reduction to reduce the federal tax burden on individual taxpayers.

As cited previously, the average American works every year until almost May to pay the government for services. Working almost a third of your life to support the political class severely restricts an individual's freedom. Thus, the second 10 percent reduction will be used solely for a permanent reduction in the federal tax burden on U.S. citizens. Of course, the political class will try to forestall this reduction by either saying the poor are not getting enough of a tax break or the rich are being asked to pay too much in taxes already, resulting in a stalemate, no tax reduction for anyone, and the loss of no power for the political class. They would win again by creating two American tribes, where the rich and the poor would fight each other and not the problem. As a result, nothing would get done and no one would be happy except for the political class that maintained the status quo.

To eliminate the probable bickering and stalemate, only the three lowest tax brackets would be reduced by 10 percent. The 15 percent bracket would become 13.5 percent, the 20 percent bracket would become 18 percent, and the 25 percent bracket would become 22.5 percent. The 28 percent, 33 percent, and 38 percent brackets, the brackets for only those earning over $79,000 a year would enter, would not be reduced.

It is a simple solution that everyone could understand without the class warfare rhetoric that would likely happen. The rich would get the advantage of lower taxes on their first $79,000 and the middle class would likely get a 10 percent reduction on everything they owed. End of story. These percentages would be a permanent, year-after-year fix. This would not be a one-time rebate-type program.

This change should not be like the benevolent mobster who gives you back a few dollars for coffee after robbing you of next month's grocery money. The change would be permanent and not subject to the whims of the political class. Remember, it is *your* money and wealth they took in the first place; it is not theirs.

> **The politicians don't just want your money. They want your soul. They want you to be worn down by taxes until you are dependent and helpless. When you subsidize poverty and failure, you get more of both."**
> —*James Dale Davidson*

Step 4

Split subsequent tax reductions fifty/fifty, with half going to further tax reductions and 50 percent used to increase funding for cancer research, AIDS research, Alzheimers research, education initiatives and drug demand reduction efforts.

The third 10 percent reduction would continue to reduce the federal tax burden on individuals, but a significant portion would be used to increase the funding for an initial, specific, and limited set of social issues. The issues would be the following:

- Research to better understand, treat, and subsequently reduce the incidence and suffering caused by breast and lung cancer, two of the biggest fatal diseases and cancers in the nation today.

- Research to better understand, treat, and subsequently reduce the incidence and suffering caused by Alzheimers/dementia, the biggest medical condition facing the country and its aging baby boomers.

- Research to better understand, treat, and subsequently reduce the incidence and suffering caused by AIDS, one of the worst diseases in the world today.

- Research and significantly improve the quality of public education in the country.

- Research and significantly reduce the negative impact of the illicit and licit drug usage in the country.

These are five of the most immediate social issues of our time; they are issues that government should be concerned about. However, the increased funding would come with requirements. Every grant under the new, incremental funding guidelines for any of the above issues would have to pass some strict but straightforward criteria that would look something like the following:

- What specific subissue is to be addressed?

- What is the expected result of the effort?

- When will that result be achieved/not be achieved?

- Who will benefit from this effort?

- How does this effort fit into the overall national effort?

- Why are you qualified to get this money?

- What are your major milestones in this effort?

Thus, no detailed plan = no money from the new funding source.

Finally, no one from the political class would be involved in distributing the funds. First, most know nothing about the five issues to begin with. Second, you can be sure they would not spend the money efficiently or effectively relative to the five issues listed. The additional money would be dispensed by one of five expert panels involved with the specific issues (i.e., oncologists for cancer, education specialists for education, etc.). These panel members would have strict but straightforward criteria for panel membership:

- Panel nomination, membership, and funding levels would be voted on by Congress. Although this is not optimal, given the inability of the political class to get anything right in a timely, efficient, and cost effective manner, the program is unlikely to become reality unless Congress has some say into how the panels would be formed.

- None of the funding would be directed to a panel member's home organization/hospital/clinic/practice or to themselves personally. This criterion would probably restrict the panel membership to experienced but retired medical and education personnel.

- Panel members would be responsible for putting together a long-term strategic plan and financial plan that integrates all efforts of each issue into an overall strategy. The plan would include specific milestones and measurements of achievement and success/failure.

- The panel would track and read out results to the nation on a semiannual basis.

- Failure to hit major milestones will result in the dissolution of the panel after five years and the establishment of a new panel.

Funding for other social issues and diseases would not be terminated but would continue under a business-as-usual scenario. This would not sit well with people suffering from other types of cancer, for instance, but for government, via the political class, to have any chance of getting something positive done, its attention must be highly focused. This is why the above five issues are the starting point—they provide a focus on the biggest challenges of our time.

In order for this step to work, it would have to be operated like a surgeon with latex gloves on and not barbecue mitts. The political class via government tries to do a little of everything today, and as a result they do everything poorly. By being strongly focused on this first, limited set of big issues, maybe they can surgically and cost-effectively make a difference in Americans' lives.

A politician is a person who can make waves and then make you think he's the only one who can save the ship.

—*Ivern Ball*

Step 5

Increase IRS and other government enforcement
efforts to recover the hundreds of billions of dollars
lost to fraud every year, including both tax fraud and
government program abuses.

The **March 4, 2008, issue** of *Money Magazine* quoted a 2006
Internal Revenue Service source, which estimated that the difference between what the IRS should have collected and what
it actually did collect in taxes from individual taxpayers was $197
billion. This means that on average, every U.S. household would
have to pay an additional $1,500 a year to cover this fraud. In addi-
tion, consider a set of small, diverse, and documented examples of
other types of government program frauds:

Amount of Fraud	Source of Information
$2,000,000 of Medicaid funds (New York)	*New York Times Online*, November 22, 2003
$142,000,000 of Medicare funds	kaisernetwork.org, May 10, 2007
$536,000 of Medicare funds (Brownsville, Texas)	oag.state.tx.us, October 19, 2005
$56,000,000 in Medicare funds (Miami)	*American Chronicle*, June 2, 2007

$462,926 in Medicaid funds (Jefferson City, Missouri)	Mathias Consulting, August, 7, 2007
$15,700,000 in Medicaid funds (Austin, Texas)	Mathias Consulting, December 7, 2006
$5,000,000 in Medicaid funds (Brownsville, Texas)	Mathias Consulting, October 24, 2006
$5,000,000 in Medicaid funds (Newark, New Jersey)	Mathias Consulting, November 14, 2006

These examples, totaling over $225,000,000, were uncovered in less than a half hour on the Internet. Imagine how many other examples there are that have been uncovered but did not make the above list and, more importantly, the fraud cases that have not yet been, and may never be, uncovered.

The political class does not worry about this type of fraud and waste since reducing it is not as glamorous as introducing new, grandiose legislation for some issue. Finding Medicare fraudsters or tax cheats does not get the headlines that other political class gestures and charades get.

However, taxpayers would appreciate any reduction in fraud and unpaid taxes since it should translate into a reduction in the tax burden on them. If income tax fraud, Medicare fraud, Social Security fraud, and other fraud could be seriously reduced, the tax implications for families would be substantial.

The first tactic under this step would be the tax auditing of every member of Congress, every cabinet secretary, the president, and the vice president, given the recent problem political class appointees (e.g. Tom Daschle, Tim Geithner) have had in filing timely and accurate tax returns. Eliminating fraud also increases the trust the average taxpayer has in the system from a fairness perspective. Once a citizen believes that he or she is being played as a sucker for paying his or her fair share, or that the members of the political class play by a different set of tax rules, the entire tax collection process becomes a sham.

Economic freedom and political freedom are attained when you keep as much of your hard-earned wealth as possible and not have it wasted via fraud and incompetence.

If con is the opposite of pro, is Congress the opposite of progress?

—author unknown

Campaign
Finance Reform

Step 6

Allow only individual citizens to contribute
to political campaigns. This eliminates the
contributions of PACs, unions, corporations, and
lobbyists. The Bill of Rights guarantees freedom of
speech for individual citizens, not groups of citizens.

One of the most hallowed and precious rights set forth in the Bill of Rights is freedom of speech. In theory, everyone's opinion counts the same, whether that person is wealthy or poor, famous or obscure, highly educated or illiterate. However, nowhere in the Bill of Rights or the Constitution does it say that organizations such as PACs, unions, corporations, or lobbyists are guaranteed freedom of speech; only individuals are. It is these organizations that have fouled most of the political processes in this country simply because they have the collective money and resources to blackmail members of the political class who are running for office.

Whenever an effort is mounted to reduce or eliminate these forces from the political process, it is these perpetrators themselves who claim that their right of free speech is being trampled, even though it is their money that drowns out the voices and opinions of the individual citizen. They have used their money to convince the political class and members of the judicial system of their position. Thus, unconscionable amounts of money flow to the political class for election. Obviously, the political class does not want this to change since they are the beneficiaries of the money flows. Also, they would claim they need these obscene amounts of money to get their message out to the public.

This proposed change, restricting campaign donations only to individual citizens, would simplify the entire campaign finance mess by returning to the roots of the country's founders: individuals are guaranteed freedom of speech, not organizations. If a politician was running for office, then any individual could exercise his or her freedom of speech by donating directly to the politician's campaign. It's that simple.

Organizations such as PACs, corporations, unions, etc., could still campaign on issues, mounting their own media efforts to advance their positions. However, they could not implicitly or explicitly endorse a candidate; they could only encourage voters/citizens to find out which politicians are in favor of their causes. They could not as an organization contribute to any candidate's campaign effort.

As for the political class's assertion that they need massive amounts of organizational donations to run their campaigns, that does not ring true in 2009. With round-the-clock news stations on TV and radio, Internet bloggers, websites, etc., there is no longer a need to run expensive political campaigns like in the past. With less money available, the candidates might actually have to make themselves available in person to their constituents, to interact with voters rather than hiding behind massive multimedia advertising programs.

Another benefit of this change is that it would level the playing field against the political class. With less money available to overwhelm new voices in the political landscape, we might actually see more diverse, and hopefully smarter and more effective, political parties and ideas rise to the public's attention. Obviously this would not sit well with the ruling political class, making this change one of the most important, but also one of the hardest to implement.

One could assert that even if this change was implemented, organizations could simply have their individual members be a front for organization donations to campaigns. This side door would obviously have to be locked by the Federal Election Commission, but it could be a simple lock. A rule would be put in place that you could not donate to any campaign more than 50 percent of your net assets. If audited, a donator would have to prove that at the time of the donation, he or she actually did not donate more than 50 percent of their net worth to the campaign. This would prevent the PACs, corporations, unions, and lobbyists from using a homeless or dead person to donate $1 million to a political campaign.

Pessimists could assert that the ultra rich could still donate megadollars to campaigns and influence policy and elections. This is true (as long as their donations were less than 50 percent of their assets), but it is also true today. At least under this proposed change, a lot, if not all, of the big dollars would be made illegal.

This step would help restore the Freedom Pyramid, where free, individual citizens drive the political process from the top of the pyramid and remove the power from special interest groups and the political class.

The government, which was designed for the people, has got into the hands of the bosses and their employees, the special interests. An invisible empire has been set up above the forms of democracy.

—*Woodrow Wilson*

Step 7

Only allow individuals to contribute to Senate or Congressional political candidates that represent them. For example, political contributions from Kansas cannot be funneled/diverted into political activities in New Jersey.

Several years ago an incumbent New Jersey senator, Democrat Robert Torricelli, was up for reelection, but got himself into a number of embarrassing predicaments that required him to terminate his campaign late in the election season. New Jersey Democrats were beside themselves, having to find a replacement for him at a very late date. They turned to Frank Lautenberg, a former U.S. senator from New Jersey to fill in, which he did, and he ended up winning Torricelli's seat.

The problem with the whole affair is that New Jersey Democrats had to consult with Tom Daschle, the current head of the political class Democrats in the Senate, and get his blessing for the substitution. At that time, New Jersey was home to approximately 8.7 million citizens while Daschle was from South Dakota, home to only 780 thousand citizens (less than 9 percent of the size of New Jersey's population according to the 2006 U.S. Census view). However, he still had veto power over the New Jersey senatorial campaign.

This incident illustrates how far we as a country have gotten away from representative government. It's the two wings of the political class that control who runs for office from each state, not the citizens of each state. Why should Daschle have to bless the Lautenberg switch? The only thing that mattered to Daschle was to get a Democrat elected, not to get the best senator for New Jersey. And while I blame the process and Daschle for the situation, it would have been nice for the Democrats in New Jersey to say they knew best for their home state and choose a replacement based on what was best for the citizens of New Jersey. Alas, they again had neither the courage nor the smarts to do the right thing.

This change is to get the political selection process back into the hands of those who should determine the elected representatives, the citizens of each state. Thus, the Howard Deans of the world would not be able to move campaign money around the country to further the aims of the political class by funding candidates that serve the parties first and the state's citizens second, if at all. In the cited example, political donations from citizens in Kansas could not be redirected to support a Senate or Congressional political campaign in New Jersey; what is donated in Kansas stays in Kansas.

The political class would hate this change. It would require them to treat every state and its citizens as an independent entity and not influence or overwhelm state campaigns with outside/national party money. In-state politicians would have to rely on their own ability to raise in-state money. If they could not raise enough, that would either mean they are incompetent fundraisers, or the citizens of that state really do not want that candidate elected, as witnessed by the lack of donations. In either case, those candidates should not be hoisted on that state's citizens because they were financially rescued with national money being directed to their campaigns.

This step would also help restore the Freedom Pyramid by allowing only a politician's constituents to have a say in the election and not be overwhelmed or overruled by distant resources.

Politics is the gentle art of getting votes from the poor and campaign funds from the rich, by promising to protect each from one another.

—*Oscar Ameringer*

Step 8

Strengthen the FEC rules and penalties and staff the commission with seasoned prosecutors, elected on a national basis, so that someone actually goes to jail once in a while for violating campaign finance laws.

Although the Federal Elections Commission (FEC) has been around since 1975, has anyone ever gone to jail as a result of its existence or had to pay a large fine for violating election laws? Despite billions of dollars flying all over the place from corporations, private citizens, PACs, foreign governments (e.g., China and the Clinton administration), a quick search on the Internet shows that the FEC has apparently never prosecuted a major violation of the federal election laws.

One reason for this track record could be that everyone is obeying the letter and spirit of the law. A more reasonable explanation is that the foxes are watching the hen house — the members of the FEC tend to be members of the political class. By rule, the Commission has to be staffed by three Democrats and three Republicans (i.e., six members from the same political class). Why then would they actively go after their own kind in the pursuit of fair election laws? As an example, look at the background of two current members of the Commission:[1]

---

1   From the FEC website, http://www.fec.gov/.

David M. Mason

- Served as senior fellow in congressional studies at the Heritage Foundation
- Served as director of executive branch liaison, director of U.S. Congress Assessment Project, and vice president, government relations, at the Heritage Foundation
- Served as assistant secretary of defense
- Served various congressional members as a legislative assistant, legislative director, and staff director
- Staff member in numerous congressional, senate, gubernatorial and presidential campaigns
- Attended Lynchburg College and graduated cum laude from Claremont McKenna College

Ellen Weintraub

- Employed as counsel to Perkins Coie LLP
- Served on the team that advised the Senate Rules Committee
- Practiced law as a litigator with the firm of Cahill, Gordon, and Reindel
- Served as counsel to the Committee on Standards of Official Conduct for the House of Representatives
- Was editor in chief of the House Ethics Manual
- Received her BA, cum laude, from Yale College and her JD from Harvard Law School

These are probably two hardworking government employees trying to do their best to track hundreds of millions of campaign dollars while insuring clean election practices. However, they have a few distressing characteristics:

1. Both appear to be long-term insiders to the political class, serving other political class members during a large part of their careers.

2. Neither of them appear to have any criminal prosecutor experience.

3. Their experience appears to be focused in facilitating political behavior (e.g., writing manuals, directing, advising, etc.) and not in tracking down and jailing lawbreakers

There needs to be a new way to staff the FEC with tough investigators and prosecutors, not political appointees. The best and only way to do that is to make the board membership a nationally elected position with members serving one six-year term. Any past member of Congress or member of a congressional staff would be barred from running and serving.

Another step to help restore the Freedom Pyramid by making sure elections and their funding are consistent with keeping the power in the hands of individual Americans.

It could probably be shown by facts and figures there is no distinctly native American criminal class except Congress.

—Mark Twain

Federal Entitlement Programs

Step 9

Make a traditional government pension plan
unavailable to all future federal government
employees, including elected representatives. They
will only have Social Security and the existing 401(k)-
like government retirement plan for their retirement
needs. In addition, all current and past members of
Congress will immediately lose access to either their
government pension or their 401(k)-like government
savings program, the choice being theirs.

According to the National Center for Policy Analysis (*Money Magazine*, March, 2008), in 2010, 8.6 percent of federal income tax revenue will be used to cover Social Security and Medicare deficits. If nothing changes, the number will grow to 76 percent of collected tax revenue by 2050. Thus, three quarters of the income tax collected will be spent before it pays a single federal employee, funds the military, or opens a national park, or before the political class funds its first pork barrel program. The current spending trajectory of the main federal entitlement programs is not sustainable. Since the political class has shown neither the courage or brains to fix the problem, the following steps need to be taken to avoid national bankruptcy.

Consider the compensation and retirement options currently available to the political class in Washington:

- Comfortable salaries that are often determined through leg-islative sleight of hand and place Congressional members in the top 5 percent of all American workers. (Source: National Tax Payer Union.)

- Wage and pension increases every year that often exceed the Consumer Price Index (CPI) while most American work-ers' pensions, if they have one, almost never rise. (Source: National Tax Payer Union)

- Pension benefits that are two to three times more generous than those offered in the private sector for similarly salaried executives, assuming that that the private sector executives have a pension. (Source: National Tax Payer Union.)

- All members of Congress receive a special tax deduction for maintaining a second residence. (Source: http://kiplinger.com, June 19, 2007.)

- All members of Congress receive free outpatient care from military hospitals. (Source: http://kiplinger.com, June 19, 2007.)

These members of the political class receive all of these benefits despite the fact that many of them are millionaires prior to com-ing into office. Thus, while most Americans do not have access to a retirement pension, those in Washington get not only a pension, but a pension that grows steadily over time even after they are out of office. While about half of American workers do not have access to a 401(k) retirement option, members of the political class partici-pate in a generous 401(k)-like plan that has high, taxpayer-funded matching contributions.

This elitist approach to rewarding the political class is bad eco-nomics and bad for the country's morale. Running for office and serving the country should not be a way to save for your retirement. Remember, according to the promise of this country, all citizens are to be treated as equals; there should not be this elite, self-enriching class of people. The fact is that most Americans not employed by the federal government will be less and less likely to have access to a pension in the future (and those who do will not likely have one that increases every year), and will have to rely on 401(k) plans and Social Security for retirement. This fact/trend should not be exclusionary for both the political class and federal workers going forward.

Now, you can just hear the political class yelling how unfair it would be for them to have to go to a less lucrative retirement plan. However, the counterargument is that there are not guarantees in life. Just ask the people at Enron and other companies whose employees lost their life savings and pensions because the Clinton SEC did not protect their investments. Ask those in the workforce who no longer have a pension because corporations have done away with them over time.

The fact that most people in the political class are quite wealthy before entering office also deflates their argument. Once they are served by the same retirement options as ordinary citizens, then we may see some meaningful reforms to get the system solvent. Additionally, this change would be retroactive, to include all members of the political class who are no longer in office, just like the collapse of pension benefits and retirement plans affected both those still in the workforce and those who are retired.

The "let them eat cake" syndrome in this country—the political class creating and living in an elite, different caste than the rest of us—has to come to an end. Under the Constitution, every citizen is entitled to the same treatment and benefits from the federal government.

The oppressed are allowed once every few years to decide which particular representatives of the oppressing class are to represent and repress them.

—Karl Marx

Step 10

Make the first $50,000 in total household income
exempt from Social Security taxes. Make up the
difference by uncapping the maximum at which
Social Security taxes will stop and change the Social
Security tax rate to 1 percent on all forms of income.

Probably the most unfair tax in the land is the Social Security tax
on wages. The amount taxed (at 6.2 percent of your wages) is
capped at $102,000, and any wages after that are not taxed at
all. Consider the following example:

Annual Wages	Amount of SS Taxes Paid	Tax As a Percentage of Wages
$102,000	$6,324	6.20 percent
$500,000	$6,324	1.26 percent
$1,000,000	$6,324	.63 percent
$10,000,000	$6,324	.06 percent

Thus, the vast majority of Americans are spending much, much
more as a percentage of others relative to their paycheck to get the
same Social Security benefit.

What would the contributions look like if we 1) uncapped the
amount taxed, by both removing the current $102,000 cap on wages
and including all earnings such as wages, interest, dividends, and

capital gains, 2) taxed all earnings at 1 percent, and 3) provided everyone with a $50,000 exemption before Social Security taxation began:

Annual Income	Amount of SS Taxes Paid	Tax as a Percentage of Earnings
$102,000	$520	.51 percent
$500,000	$4,500	.90 percent
$1,000,000	$9,500	.95 percent
$10,000,000	$99,500	1.00 percent

There are multiple benefits of this approach:

- As a percentage of income, the difference is much fairer.

- It is possible that more money may be collected in this scenario than the current environment, helping the solvency of the entire system.

- Millions of lower-income U.S. households would have substantially more money in their pockets from the reduced Social Security taxes, resulting in a great stimulus to the economy.

- A 1 percent tax on all income is not very onerous, particularly on those who can afford it.

- It would postpone the long-term need to reform the entire tax system, which the political class has shown they are unable to do. Having extra money in the pockets of those at the lower-income scale from this change is as good as changing the income tax code. Who cares where the extra money comes from—it's all the same to the taxpayer. Thus, the majority of Americans get a tax break and the system gets more solvent at the same time without the usual debate and failure about reforming the tax code.

Obviously, those who would pay more in Social Security taxes would be likely to oppose this fundamental change and would appeal to the political class, which contains many millionaires who may also oppose the changes. However, if you are going to have a Social Security system and you want to keep it solvent, change is necessary, and continuing to burden those at the lower income levels with a disproportionately higher percentage of taxation will not be enough.

As an example, consider a millionaire earner, not a figure unheard of these days. In the current system he would pay $6,324 in Social Security taxes, or about $527 a month. Under the proposed scenario, he would pay about $792 a month, an increase of $265 a month. However, at $1,000,000 he is earning $83,333 a month, which would then drop to $83,068 a month. Hardly a reason to sell the summer house or the yacht.

The business contribution side of the equation would remain the same. No need to make this whole process more complicated than it should be (and thus increasing the chance it will never happen). Businesses know how to pay their share of the Social Security tax for their employees and that would continue as is, saving them administrative resources that would be needed to change this side of the equation.

Again, the whole emphasis of this book is to get government out of everyone's life, including the lives of the rich. However, if the Social Security system is to continue, it must be fixed soon and be made fairer. Smarter people than me can haggle over the proposed parameters. Maybe the exemption should be $30,000 and the tax rate 1.5 percent or some other combination. Maybe the numbers should vary over time depending on where we are with the aging of the baby boomers. However, the overall strategy should not change: make the system solvent now, do it fairly across the board, and make it a nonissue for the political class to exploit.

Economic freedom = political freedom. This single change in the tax system would result in the largest increase in economic freedom for the most Americans ever.

The nation should have a tax system that looks like someone designed it on purpose.

—*William Simon*

Step 11

Prohibit citizens with more than $3,000,000 in assets (not income) from drawing any Social Security checks until such time that they have less than $3,000,000 in assets.

Lets assume that you are sixty-five years old have $3,000,000 in assets (not income) that earn about 5 percent a year; the earnings are easily attained at little risk with investments weighted toward T-bills, with a little bit of stock and real estate investments thrown in. Thus, a 5 percent return generates $150,000 a year in income. Most people could live very comfortably on $150,000 a year, $12,500 a month, particularly if they have paid down their mortgage, educated their children, and married them off, likely scenarios at age sixty-five. This level of income would put you into the upper 5 to 6 percent of the general population from an income perspective (U.S. Census, 2005) and it would leave your principal unchanged, continuing to support your future living needs.

If you were to no longer receive a Social Security check for the average amount, about $1,200 a month, you would not likely see a significant drop in your lifestyle, starve, or go homeless. For every person in this $3 million-and-above wealth range who does not receive a Social Security check, there is another, less fortunate person who has a better chance of continuing to receive a steady, stable Social Security check to survive.

Bottom line: there is absolutely no reason why the solvency of the entire system should be endangered by continuing to send money to the likes of Bill Gates, Donald Trump, and the other top wealth holders in this country. Social Security should be a lifeline for those that are less fortunate; it should not be a reward for those who can afford to live without the check.

This is a prime example where latex gloves are much better and more elegant than the oven mitts that the current Social Security System uses. Basing payouts on need would make the system more solvent and last longer while not depriving millionaires of a viable living standard.

> **I care about our young people and I wish them great success. Because they are our hope for the future and some day, when my generation retires, they will pay us trillions of dollars in Social Security.**
>
> —*Dave Barry*

Step 12

Increase the retirement age over time, bringing it to seventy within ten years.

This is an easy fix that, when executed with the above fixes, would save the entire Social Security system. Through advancements in medicine, better knowledge of healthy eating habits, reduced smoking levels, safer cars, etc., the average lifespan of an American has increased dramatically from when Social Security was first introduced. Data from an article on Social Security in *Time Magazine* from March 20, 1995, illustrates this point perfectly:

- In 1940, 54 percent of U.S. men and 61 percent of U.S. women could expect to reach their sixty-fifth birthday.

- By 1990, 72 percent of men and 84 percent of women could expect to reach their sixty-fifth birthday.

- In 1950 there were sixteen workers paying into the Social Security System for every retired worker drawing benefits.

- By 2030 there will be only two workers paying into the Social Security System for every retired worker drawing benefits.

Given the changing environment, the retirement age should rise also, putting less strain on the system. Those who cannot afford to wait for a later retirement could apply for early benefits.

However, those people with a comfortable asset level would have to wait until seventy.

The above three changes, steps 10, 11, and 12, would help save the system later and stimulate the economy now. But more importantly, it would take the Social Security issue out of play for the political class, who would otherwise use it to pit one group of citizens against another, helping to perpetuate their run in office.

Latex gloves would allow for more precision in getting limited Social Security funds only to those who need them.

Age is an issue of mind over matter. If you don't mind, it doesn't matter.

—Mark Twain

Voting

Step 13

Stop funding political conventions with taxpayer dollars. All costs, including security costs, will be the responsibility of each political party.

ong ago, presidential candidates were selected at their respective party's national convention. At this convention, delegates from every state attended a multiday convention to hear speeches and endorsements, write and vote on the party's platform, attend pep rallies, and party for several days. During the course of the convention, votes were taken to determine who the party's next presidential candidate would be.

However, that process no longer exists, having been replaced by the primary and caucus system. Prior to the convention, states conduct elections to determine who will win the delegate votes from their state. Thus, when the delegates attend the convention they are merely rubberstamping the results of the primary and caucus voters. In recent memory, the candidate to be nominated by the major parties was predetermined prior to the convention, since they had won enough delegates through the state primary system to meet the criteria for nomination.

Thus, there is no reason anymore to hold a convention to pick a candidate. The convention system is now merely a three-to-four day excuse to rally the troops, listen to speeches and endorsements, and to party. Unfortunately, the American taxpayer now pays for this private party and it is not a paltry sum. As a result of the 9-11 attacks and the increased threat of terrorism, the federal cost to the American taxpayer for the 2004 conventions was in excess of $100 million. If the political class still wants to have conventions, then they should go right ahead and have them, but pay for them out of their own funds. Since there is no reason to pick a candidate at the convention, their primary purpose has vanished.

Think about how the spending of $100 million on the conventions could be better spent (source of costs analysis: *Parade Magazine*, "Better Ways to Spend a Billion Dollars"):

- hiring almost 2,400 additional teachers for a year

- paying for basic health insurance for 25,000 Americans

- buying 41.5 million school lunches for needy children.

Sounds a lot like the "Let Them Eat Cake" vignette —"We are throwing a party for ourselves, you are not invited, and you have to pay for it. Also, we will be preempting your favorite TV shows in the process."

Politics, n: [Poly "many" + tics "blood sucking parasites"]
—*Larry Hardiman or Gore Vidal (conflicting sources)*

Step 14

Stop configuring Congressional voting districts to almost guarantee the reelection of incumbents.

Gerrymander: to divide a state, county, or city into voting districts to give an unfair advantage to one party in elections.

Shortly after the 2000 census, the *Newark Star Ledger* paper reported that the two wings of the New Jersey political class had redistricted/gerrymandered the state so that it was virtually impossible for the Democrats not to have seven Congressional seats and the Republicans not to have six Congressional seats from New Jersey. This was accomplished by using a very contorted and convoluted approach to drawing up Congressional districts:

- A long skinny Republican district (District 5) stretches across the state, beginning in the northeast corner of the state, running along the top of the state to the northwest corner, and then making an abrupt left-hand turn down the western edge of the state.

- District 7 was deemed to be another Republican district, and it stretches and meanders aimlessly from the western edge of New Jersey across four counties, almost reaching New York City at its eastern edge.

- District 12 was deemed to be a Democrat district, and it has an even funkier shape than District 7. It crosses five New Jersey counties (almost 25 percent of all state counties) and runs from the Delaware River on the western state line all the way across the state to the Atlantic Ocean. Its boundaries also meander up and down, east and west, according to the agreed to plan, to make sure it is a Democrat district.

- District 6 is not even contiguous; you have to cross district lines to go from one part of District 6 to another part of District 6!

The Republican voters in District 12 basically have no say in who their elected officials are, since their district has been deemed a Democrat district and configured so that it is overwhelmingly Democrat. Conversely, Democrats in District 5 have no say in who their elected officials are since that district has been rigged to be a Republican district.

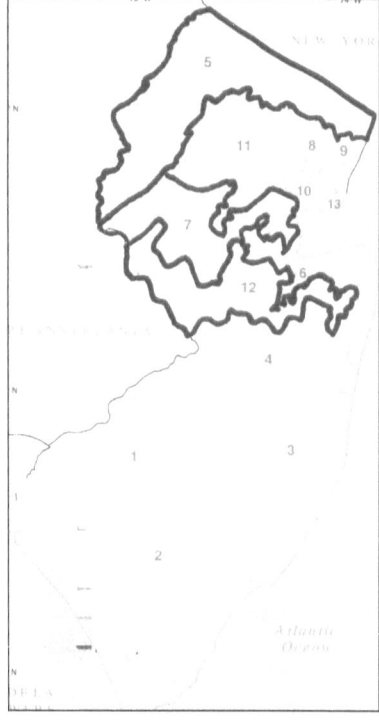

By doing this gerrymandering, the political class in New Jersey basically disenfranchised thousands and thousands of New Jersey voters.

Besides disenfranchising these citizens, by focusing voter blocks together, we now tend to get politicians that represent more extreme viewpoints, since their sending districts have been configured for certain political blocs. Rather than building consensus and developing compromises, we end up with Washington gridlock because the elected officials have such a focused home district.

Disenfranchisement, political gridlock, extreme positions on issues, etc., all make for lousy government and lousy politicians. Thus, new redistricting rules must be implemented when future redistricting needs to be done:

- Voting districts should not include more than two counties (unless the two counties do not have a sufficient number of residents). District 12 in New Jersey unnecessarily stretches across five New Jersey counties, almost 25 percent of the total number of counties in New Jersey.

- The widest geographic diameter of a district should be no more than three times the length of the smallest geographic dimension. This would eliminate the formation of voting districts that are stretched in various directions and contortions to get the right mix according to the wishes of the political class.

- And most importantly, no active or former member of the political class should be involved in the formulation of the voting districts. They have proven that they cannot resist the temptation to gerrymander, and there is no reason to think they would stop in the future. Voting redistricting would be run by independent panels with no stake in the outcome of the district formulation. One approach that could be used would be to have the redistricitng done by people from outside the state. For instance, a panel from North Dakota, using precise, non-politically motivated criteria, could draw up Florida's new districts. If need be, the function could be outsourced to foreigners—whatever it takes to keep the political class out of the process.

All votes should carry the same amount of weight, something not currently happening in this country. This change would go a long way to restoring the freedom pyramid and returning power to each American.

> **Apparently, a democracy is a place where numerous elections are held at great cost without issues and with interchangeable candidates.**
>
> —*Gore Vidal*

Step 15

For all presidential debates, include any candidates that have a mathematical chance of winning the election.

What came first, the chicken or the egg? Do third party candidates never win presidential races because they are not included in the debates, or do they not get invited to debates because they never win elections? Once the two wings of the single political class have their nominees, they are matched up in a series of highly rigid, uninformative events called debates. A debate is defined as a formal discussion or argument. Presidential debates are two folks answering questions from a moderator, rarely engaging in any kind of argument or meaningful debate.

Why isn't there ever any lively repartee? Because both major party candidates differ only around the edges when it comes to policy and governing. Remember, they may be different parties, but they both belong to the political class, whose priorities are to get elected and gain power, not to improve the country. Thus, our favorite TV shows are canceled again for no real gain.

Future presidential debates should include candidates from all parties that have a mathematical chance to win the election; that is, they are on enough ballots across the states to theoretically get enough electoral college votes to win. Thus, the Green Party and Ralph Nader would have been present in 2000 to join in the debates, as would have Harry Browne of the Libertarian Party, Howard Phillips of the Constitution Party, David McReynolds of the Socialist Party, etc. Now that would have made for a much more honest exchange of ideas and open discussion than watching the Gore/Bush and Bush/Kerry robothons. Opening up the debates would have made for franker political discussion and allowed for a freer flow of ideas not controlled by the political class.

The political class loves to the control the debates since it diverts attention from the real issues, just like Oceania diverted attention from its issues by constantly warring with Eurasia and Eastasia. So why listen to commentary on who "won" the debate, who wore what at the debate, who had a hidden microphone at the debate, etc.? Real issues and problems are not addressed; maintaining the status quo and the political class rule is the objective.

Once a government is committed to the principle of silencing the voice of opposition, it has only one way to go, and that is down the path of increasingly repressive measures, until it becomes a source of terror to all its citizens and creates a country where everyone lives in fear.

—Harry Truman

Step 16

Scrap the electoral college and elect presidents by popular vote only.

Besides the hassle of modifying the Constitution to make this change, can anyone explain why this feature of the election process still needs to exist? If we are to believe that everyone's vote has equal weight, then we need to elect our presidents by the popular vote count in the future, not by the antiquated electoral college. I am sure that Al Gore fans would agree with this change based on their belief that Gore won the popular vote in 2000 but still did not get elected president.

However, there is a more important reason to change this process. If you live in Massachusetts and are a Republican, your vote for president is usually worthless. Since 1940, Massachusetts has almost always voted Democrat for president, and thus all of the Massachusetts electoral votes have gone to the Democrats over those years. (Source: U.S. Election Atlas). Your Republican vote in that state would almost never make a difference, as it is lost and overwhelmed when the entire state votes Democrat and the all-or-nothing setup passes all of the electoral votes to the Democrats.

Similarly, if you are a Democrat in Kansas, your vote is also usually worthless. That state has voted Republican all but once since 1940 (Johnson in 1964). Your vote is lost when all of the electoral votes go to the Republicans.

As a short-term solution prior to modifying the Constitution, states should be encouraged to follow the model currently in place in Nebraska and Iowa. In those states, electoral votes are allocated based on the percentage of votes that go to each candidate, based on how many districts each candidate wins. (Colorado attempted to move to a similar format, but it was defeated on a referendum). If the Democrats win 60 percent of the districts in Nebraska or Iowa, they get 60 percent of the electoral votes and the Republicans get 40 percent. The Democrats would not win the traditional 100 percent. This setup adds value to everyone's vote regardless of what party they vote for and what state they are in since the electoral vote assignment is closer to the actual popular vote.

Furthermore, not all electoral college votes are created equal. Given how the number of electoral college votes are determined, electoral votes in some states have more than three times the value of electoral votes in other states. For example, if you take the number of electoral votes in six states—Texas, Florida, California, Vermont, Washington DC, and Wyoming—and calculate the ratio of electoral votes per 100,000 people in each state's population, you would get the following ratios:

- 0.1398 votes per 100,000 Texans

- 0.1473 votes per 100,000 Floridians

- 0.1496 votes per 100,000 Californians

- 0.4829 votes per 100,000 Vermonters

- 0.5069 votes per 100,000 DC residents

- 0.5632 votes per 100,000 Wyoming residents

Thus, Wyoming has the best value relative to electoral votes—more than four times more powerful, based on state population, than the worst valued electoral votes in Texas.

The political class would probably object to this change, for the same reason mentioned many times before: they would lose power to control if a change was made, ceding their current concentration of power to the voters. In the last several elections, very few Democratic Party presidential candidates spent any significant amount of time in New Jersey. Why? Polls accurately showed that New Jersey would almost always vote heavily for the Democrats.

The political class then spent very little time in those states where the outcome was more or less predetermined, focusing only on those states that could go either way. As a result, fewer and fewer states get to hear from and interact with the candidates, depriving the residents of those states a fair way to have input into the campaigns. By getting rid of the electoral college, the political class would be forced to engage all of the citizens on an equal basis, since everyone's vote would count for something again.

This is another example of where the freedom pyramid concept has become inverted and needs to revert back to where the individual citizen rules through his or her vote, a vote that does not get marginalized by the electoral college math.

Politicians are like diapers. They both need changing regularly and for the same reason.

—author unknown

Step 17

Eliminate the Democratic Party's so-called "super delegates" process, allowing citizens' voting in the primaries to be the direct cause of a candidate's selection.

The Democrats have an interesting twist to their primary elections process. Although the primaries are supposed to reflect the will of the people voting by determining how many delegates each candidate will get, based on how well the vote went for them, the Democrats add an extra layer of control called the "super delegates." These super delegates, which comprise about 20 percent of the total number of delegates at the convention, are not bound by any voice of the people. They are allowed to go the convention and vote for whoever they want to regardless of how well the candidates did in the primary elections.

And who are these super delegates? They are Democratic Party insiders, high-ranking members of the elite political class. They include currently serving Democratic members of Congress, current Democratic governors, and elder political class members such as Al Gore, Bill Clinton, and Jimmy Carter. And why do they exist? According to Meredith McGehee of the Campaign Legal Center (as quoted in *The Week*, March 7, 2008): "There was a view that the Democratic Party had allowed the grass roots to become too empowered, and that people whose job it was to get Democrats elected were being shut out."

Thus, according to McGehee and others, the job description of a super delegate could be translated as follows:

- We do not want the grass roots of the country (i.e., individual citizens), to become too empowered, so we have to have veto power over their choices.

- It is not important that the people get what they want; the overriding aim is to get our fellow political class members elected.

With 20 percent of the voting power at their disposal, the super delegates can negate any sense of the democratic process as exercised through the primary elections. The power brokers can bribe, cajole, intimidate, and/or coerce a small number of super delegates in a convention back room to overturn the voting choices of millions and the entire primary election process.

Since when can the grass roots/ordinary citizens become "too empowered?" The thought should put shivers down any freedom-loving American's spine. The super delegate concept is no more than another power grab by the political class and should be denounced and eliminated immediately.

The presence and power of super delegates represents one of the most damaging and repugnant concepts that exists in America today. It is the reincarnation of the USSR's Politburo, an elite class of insiders that ran everything as they saw fit without the nuisance of the citizenry's opinions, a concept at odds with the Freedom Pyramid ideal.

> **Political language—and with variations this is true of all political parties, from Conservatives to Anarchists—is designed to make lies sound truthful and murder respectable, and to give an appearance of solidity to pure wind.**
>
> —*George Orwell*

Step 18

Hold all Republican and Democrat primaries on the same Saturday date in late April.

I n 2000, neither party was running an incumbent for president, and each party had to find a person to run via the primary system. Living in New Jersey at that time meant that I would get to vote for a candidate in June. I was personally interested in seeing John McCain get the Republican nomination and Bill Bradley get the Democrat nomination. However, by the time that June came around, Bush had sewn up the Republican nomination and Gore had sewn up the Democrats' nomination. While I still got to vote in the New Jersey primary, it did not matter since everything was already determined.

That same scenario played out again in Florida in 2008. Tired of having their votes not count in selecting a candidate, Florida state politicians decided to move up their primary election so they would be a factor in selecting the next presidential candidate. Rather than allowing Iowa and New Hampshire, whose combined population is less than 24 percent of Florida's population, have a disproportionate share of weight in selecting a candidate, Florida moved up its primary by several months.

And how did the political class respond to Florida citizens having a fair say in the primary system? The Democrats boycotted the state, vowing not to campaign there or seat the Florida delegation at the convention. The reason is quite simple: by spacing out the elections to their liking, the political class can control the nomination process through the primary schedule. Rather than let each citizen, regardless of what state they live in, decide who should run for president, they control who votes when, and if some voters never get a real chance to vote for the candidates they want, then so be it.

People have criticized this proposed change, saying candidates would never campaign in the smaller states if it was implemented. This is probably true to some degree, but did it make sense in 2000 to have Iowa and New Hampshire help decide who the candidates would be while disenfranchising the whole state of New Jersey, which had more than twice as many citizens? Did it make sense to cut Florida out of the run up to the 2008 election because they wanted their citizens to have real input?

There should be a national primary day in April, where everyone votes in the national primary if they want to, and every citizen who votes has an equal say in who gets nominated regardless of what state they reside in. Untold millions of dollars would be saved by shortening the primary season, since the numerous candidates would not be spending millions of campaign dollars once the national primary day was over, and hopefully some of that money would find its way to better uses.

And why does an election always have to be on a Tuesday? With more and more voters not turning out to vote because of their disgust with the single political class, everything should be done to make voting easier, and by holding the national primary (and other elections) on a Saturday, you remove an obstacle to the apathetic not voting (e.g., I worked late, I was too busy picking up the kids, etc). However, I would bet that the fewer voters that come out to vote, the happier the political class is, since they have more control over the process, and they can get their die-hard supporters out without worrying about the greater good.

"Let them eat cake": we (the political class) control the nomination process, and we will determine whether or not you get a true vote in selecting the candidates.

Every election is a sort of advance auction sale of stolen goods.

—Henry Louis Mencken

Eminent Domain

Step 19

Make it illegal for any government entity to condemn your land and/or homestead for the purpose of turning it over or selling it to private commercial interests, regardless of the perceived "public good."

I n 2006, the United States Supreme Court ruled in the *Kelo* versus *New London* case that the city of New London had the right, under eminent domain, to force the sale of citizens' homes and hand that property over to private developers for the "public good." Traditionally, eminent domain was only used to take property, for a theoretically fair market price, and use the land for schools, roads, bridges, and other public works. This case allowed New London to hand the property to developers who in turn would build private offices, homes, and other commercial buildings in the hope of improving the local economy.

At first glance, the New London intentions seem worthwhile: take a somewhat rundown area and try to spark an economic success story. However, in reality, this becomes a very slippery slope in many ways. Who is to say what is a "public good" when it comes to private development? A member of the political class who may or may not have received campaign donations from a local developer? What happens when a member of the political class has a beef with a private citizen? Can they then try to uproot and destroy this person's life via an eminent domain/public good play?

Consider Monmouth County, New Jersey. In 2005, in a series of federal law enforcement raids, eleven politicians, including sitting mayors, councilmen, and judges, were arrested after being indicted for widespread illegal kickbacks and bribes. Most of the offenses were related to dealing with people and companies in the development/construction arena. The number of arrested officials eventually rose to eighteen, and their cases are currently going through the judicial process. It is a small step from taking a bribe to fix a school or build a road to taking a bribe to expel someone from their home under this Kelo definition of eminent domain.

The affected people in New London did not want to give up their homes. The government in New London decided that they had to because it was for the public good as they, the politicians, saw it. Their homes should have been sacred and untouchable relative to some developer's plans. It is where they raised their children, celebrated family events, and assumed that they had a piece of the American dream until some politician said get out. And now the Supreme Court has made it acceptable for any member(s) of the political class to do it to any other American.

Thus, what is needed is a national law that clearly states that United States citizens have the right to stay in their homes regardless of what some local politician thinks is best for the "public good" unless that public good is a government necessity such as a road, bridge, school, etc. In other words, it should be unlawful and forbidden to transfer lands seized by eminent domain to a private entity.

This situation is really a freedom pyramid issue. If you cannot control what happens to your home, what can you control?

Each of us has the natural right—from God—to defend his person, his liberty, and his property. These are the three basic requirements of life, and the preservation of any one of them is completely dependent upon the preservation of the other two. For what are our faculties but the extension of our individuality? And what is property but an extension of our faculties?

—*Frederic Bastiat*

Patriot Act

Step 20

Determine the effectiveness of each part of the Patriot Act. An independent panel will conduct a comprehensive review, then propose whatever changes to the act it deems necessary to balance security with freedom. A national referendum will vote on the proposed changes.

The Patriot Act, a misnomer if there ever was one, was enacted as a result of the 9-11 terrorist attacks. It provides significant leeway in the areas of surveillance and apprehension of both U.S. citizens and noncitizens for the prevention of further terrorist attacks. While it may have prevented further attacks, many believe it has significantly trampled the privacy rights and constitutional rights of all American citizens.

Despite this potential trampling of rights, few members of the political class have had the courage to speak out against it lest they be viewed as weak on terrorism. Better to have rights violated than lose an election seems to be their motto. Thus, they cannot be trusted to take an unbiased, hard review of the act to determine the delicate balance of freedom versus terrorism.

This change would remove that decision from their hands. Congress would appoint an independent panel that would have the highest security clearance possible to delve into what the act has done and prevented, as the political class has not had the courage to share with the American public what plots, if any, have been thwarted by the act. The panel would consist of military, economic, legal, foreign affairs, and civil libertarian experts who can present a balanced analysis and a serious set of alternatives to the act. These alternatives would then be put to a vote by the American public. They are the best judges of how much freedom they should give up for security, not the political class.

If ever there was a governmental five-legged dog, the Patriot Act is it. Just because you call it patriotic to have your rights sapped and disregarded does not mean it is patriotic.

Those who would give up essential liberty to purchase a little temporary safety, deserve neither liberty nor safety.
—Ben Franklin

Step 21

Make it illegal to tap the phones, intercept the mail, monitor the Internet activity, or examine the library and phone records of any U.S. citizen without a warrant that shows probable cause.

Prior to the convening of the Patriot Act review panel, a short-term immediate fix is to change the law such that no United States citizen can be investigated by *any* government agency without a judge-approved warrant being obtained. This right has been so basic to American freedom for so long that it is a disgrace that it no longer exists. By requiring a warrant for any United States citizen investigation, the checks and balances that are so vital to maintaining American freedoms are restored.

This would require that law enforcement do more work to prove to a judge that there is a high probability of lawbreaking going on. Law enforcement would not be allowed to go on a fishing expedition or to harass citizens without doing their due diligence. It's more work, but it is the price to be paid in a democratic country. No warrant = no investigation.

Five Legged Dog Part II – it can never be "patriotic" in this country to invade a citizen's privacy without a valid warrant.

Good people do not need laws to tell them to act responsibly, while bad people will find a way around the laws.

—Plato

Step 22

Require that the government, at the end of any
phone-tapping activities, mail interception, etc.,
tell a vindicated citizen what information the
government collected and why.

To prevent further erosion of rights, an additional checkpoint
should be implemented to further protect the rights of United
States citizens. If a citizen has been investigated, legally through
a warrant process or illegally through some rogue investigation,
and is found to be not guilty of any misdoings, the investigating
organization should be required to inform the citizen of the investigation and be told what information was collected as a result of that
investigation. A citizen who did nothing wrong deserves to know
what dossier has been compiled on him or her. This would serve
to deter illegal behavior by the government and political class by
making them reveal what they have been doing in secrecy, even if
their efforts found no wrongdoings.

Five Legged Dog Part III – it should never be "patriotic" for any
government agency to secretly maintain files about innocent citizens
without that citizen knowing what information has been collected.

A government that is big enough to give you all you want is big enough to take it all away.

—Barry Goldwater

Energy Independence

Step 23

Develop a rational, national strategic energy plan with four interlocking goals: energy will be cheaper, energy will be primarily domestically produced, energy will be cleaner, and energy will be more diversified.

The current energy crisis really began in the early 1970s with the first Arab oil embargo. Over the last thirty-five years the political class has been working (or not working, based on their lack of progress) to come up with a viable national energy policy and strategy. This thirty-five years covered periods when both the Republicans and Democrats were in charge of the White House and both parts of Congress. After more than thirty years of trying, it is my understanding that the United States energy strategy consists of the following components:

1. Bribe Iowa corn farmers to raise more corn, and to divert new and existing corn crops to the production of corn ethanol, by providing subsidies and enacting tariffs on imported ethanol.

2. Change daylight saving time.

3. Increase average car gas mileage rates far down the road (i.e., "after I am out of office") in the year 2020.

After thirty-five years this is the best the political class has been able to come with! In fact, the country does not have a coherent energy strategy and it is resulting in increasingly expensive energy costs for consumers and businesses, inflationary pressures on food, growing dependence on nondomestic sources of energy, and record high profits for oil companies.

Several years ago when gasoline prices first started breaking through the three dollars a gallon range, remember what the political class's reaction was? I still remember the politicians going out and standing in front of gas stations to express their outrage, proposing that Congress enact a bill to send one hundred dollars to everyone to help pay for the increased gas prices. This is not a strategic plan, it is a public relations stunt.

A strategic plan has a set of distinct components, including:

1. Identifying a better place where you want to be

2. Defining and *understanding* the problem or the situation you are currently in

3. Proposing how to get from where you are to where you want to be.

It's not too hard for most people to come up with a strategic plan, but it is possibly beyond the political class if, after thirty-five years, we are left with bribing corn farmers and getting up in the dark for an energy plan. And even this plan is flawed if you review some of the latest positions on ethanol-based corn fuels. Consider the views of Cornell professor of ecology David Pimentel, who made the following assertions in *Natural Resources Research* (Volume 12, No. 2), laying out the dubious economics of corn based ethanol:

- Gasohol (ethanol and gas mix) costs more at the pump but delivers poorer mileage because ethanol has only two-thirds the energy content of a comparable amount of gasoline.

- U.S. ethanol production is subsidized by the federal government (and United States taxpayers) by $1.4 billion a year.

- The push for corn-based ethanol has resulted in corn crops being diverted from the food stream, pushing up food prices around the world.

- Making a gallon of ethanol from corn requires 29 percent more energy from fossil fuels than a gallon of ethanol can provide.

- Corn farming in general takes a terrible toll on the environment, causing soil erosion and requiring more herbicides and nitrogen fertilizer than any other crop.

Professor Pimentel is not a lone wolf crying out against the use of corn ethanol for fuel. Both mainstream and specialty publications have laid out the case against the use of corn ethanol over the past few years. One of the most recent publications is the *Time* magazine April 7, 2008, issue whose cover story was entitled the "Clean Energy Myth." In this issue, *Time* asserts that:

- Biofuels like corn-based ethanol are driving up food prices

- Biofuels are making global warming worse

- The United States taxpayer is footing the bill, via subsidies, for the increase in food prices and the increase in global warming.

Apparently, though, the political class never got around to reading any of them.

IDENTIFYING WHERE WE WANT TO BE
A strategic energy plan might look something like the following:

A rational, national strategic energy plan with four interlocking goals will be developed: energy will be cheaper, energy will be primarily domestically produced, energy will be cleaner, and energy will be more diversified.

This strategy would look like the following diagram:

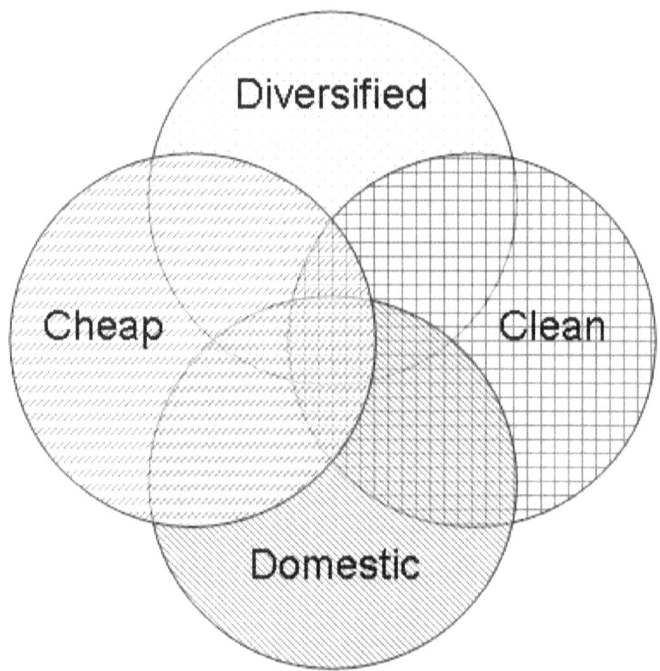

The objective would be to develop as many energy sources and programs as possible that landed toward the center of the diagram, hopefully falling within at least two of the criteria (e.g., solar energy programs might fall both in the "domestically produced" bubble and the "cleaner" bubble). Energy ideas and programs that fell into one bubble or had a detrimental effect on the other bubbles would be not favored by the new strategy.

Defining and Understanding the Problem or the Situation

We would need to summarize where we are relative to where we want to go. It is pretty obvious what the current situation is: the United States is too dependent on energy sources that originate in other parts of a sometimes hostile world. This has resulted in higher and higher prices, as well as potential supply shortfalls that have dire economic implications. The current energy policies are also too focused on CO_2-emitting sources that cause pollution and possibly global warming.

Understanding the problem is key to solving the problem. A number of interrelated issues need to be addressed and integrated into the path to solving the energy crisis:

- Technology—current and potential

- Tax laws and their impact

- Environment laws and their impact

- Infrastructure

- Economics

- Foreign affairs and international relationships

- Raw material availability

- Costs

- Timelines and milestones

The political class has done none of this understanding work, judging by their inadequate energy policy for the nation.

PROPOSING A PATH FROM WHERE WE ARE TO WHERE WE WANT TO BE

Once we can define and understand our current strategic situation, we then pick a path that will lead us out of the current and toward the ideal. This step consists of a number of tactics that will be used based on our understanding of where we want to get to. For energy it could look similar to the following:

- By 2020, renewable sources of energy (solar, wind geothermal) will provide x percent of the country's energy, up from y percent today.

- By 2020, hydrogen sources will provide w percent of the country's energy, up from z percent today.

- By 2020, clean burning domestic coal will account for twice as much of the energy than it does today.

- Etc., etc., etc.

In order for a strategic plan to work, the path must be detailed, definitive, urgent, and measurable. Thus, it needs dates, target levels, and measurable milestones with accountability for each milestone assigned. Strategic planning is not hard if you know how to put a plan together.

Now compare this hypothetical strategic plan proposed above from someone who knows very little about energy and compare it to the current national energy program:

1. Bribe Iowa farmers to raise more corn, and divert new and existing corn crops to the production of corn ethanol, by providing subsidies and enacting tariffs on imported ethanol.

2. Change daylight saving time

3. Increase average car gas mileage rates a few decades down the road.

Not much of a comparison. There is no timeline, accountability, urgency, etc., for solving this national dilemma.

Thus, to initiate this change, this step proposes that a panel consisting of experts from across the country be assembled to come up with a coherent, detailed, national strategic energy plan. This panel would be appointed by Congress but would be independent of their influence. Members would consist of subject matter experts from all types of energy sources along with sociologists, economists, and foreign experts who could provide insights of how other countries' energy strategies are laid out.

Their job would be to come up with two to three viable, very detailed long-term energy plans, along with the upsides and downsides of each plan, detailed timelines and milestones, and the related costs, which would then be voted on by the American citizens in a national election. The political class would not decide which plan to pursue. These different plans could hypothetically look like the following:

- Hydrogen focus: convert the current energy superstructure and fuel from oil-based to hydrogen-based over the next twenty years.

- Renewable focus: make wind, solar, hydro, and other renewable sources the dominant energy driver over the next twenty years.

- Diversity focus: diversify national energy consumption so that oil, coal, hydrogen, and renewables generate about the same percentage of national energy needs within twenty years.

The political class would not decide which plan to pursue. They are no better or more qualified at deciding energy policy than the typical American citizen.

A five -legged dog example: saying you have an energy policy, especially when it consists only of bribing corn farmers, changing daylight saving time, and changing car mileage requirements in the distant future, does not make it a viable strategy.

A politician looks forward only to the next election. A statesman looks forward to the next generation.
— *Thomas Jefferson*

Step 24

Institute a national research program to find a way to economically clean up coal as an energy source.

Although the political class through government institutions has accomplished very little in the past twenty years, this may be one area that they may serve a purpose. Although coal is one of the dirtiest energy sources around, it is also the most abundant and the cheapest, despite what Al Gore may have to say about its impact on global warming. It is here to stay and is likely to become more and more prevalent. The amount of oil and natural gas in the world is now measured in decades, but the amount of coal in the world is still measured in centuries. Coal is not likely going away as a worldwide and widely used energy source.

While important to our energy uses, it is the cheapest and most abundant source of energy in the fastest growing countries around the world: China, India, and Brazil. These countries are unlikely to sacrifice cheap energy that fuels their economic growth because of global warming. Add in the fact that these countries' expanded use of coal makes them less reliant on the unstable sources of oil from the Middle East.

Thus, rather than try to do the impossible, get coal out of the equation, efforts should be focused on how to make coal a better source of energy from an environmental perspective. The model would follow along the lines of the Manhattan Project, a very focused, results-oriented project that the United States undertook to develop the atomic bomb. The government would fund the research but then get out of the way, just as in the Manhattan Project, to let the scientists do their thing. Their only job would be to develop economic ways to significantly reduce the emissions of greenhouse gases that result from burning coal for energy.

They may come up with any number of both short-term and long-term ways to get rid of the "bad stuff" coal produces. Whether they would be successful is unknown. However, not trying is not an option. Coal is here to stay, both economically and politically, so a focused effort is needed to make it work. Cutting back subsidies to the oil industry would be a first step in funding the research effort, along with matching funding from the coal industry.

An interesting side note to the whole coal debate is that the federal government, even while many politicians have hopped upon the global warming and carbon emissions bandwagon, continues to use taxpayer money to support the proliferation of coal-fired, carbon-spewing power plants across America. According to a May 14, 2007 *Washington Post* article, published in the St. Petersburg Times:

- A Depression-era program, the Rural Utilities Service, designed to bring electricity to rural areas, is using taxpayer money to provide billions of dollars in low-interest loans to build coal plants even as Congress seeks ways to limit greenhouse emissions.

- The nation's rural electric cooperatives plan to spend $35 billion to build conventional coal plants over the next ten years under the program.

- These coal plants would be enough to offset all state and federal efforts to reduce U.S. greenhouse gas emissions over that time.

Thus, making coal clean is an energy and environment must.

It is obvious that the government and the ruling political class have been using barbecue mitts to manage the energy needs of the country over the past three decades, with disastrous results. We need a surgical precision approach to unlock the potential of coal from both an economic and clean air perspective.

> **Smell that—you hardly smell anything. This is a clean fuel, converted from coal by a chemical process. We can produce enough of this in Montana to power every car in America for decades.**
>
> *—Brian Schweitzer*

Step 25

Immediately assert diplomatic pressure on China
and India to develop and implement clean energy
initiatives that significantly reduce the current and
future carbon dioxide footprint in their economies.
The federal government, along with other
concerned countries, will be responsible for this.

According to Fareed Zakara of *Newsweek* in his April 16, 2007, article, "The Case for a Global Carbon Tax," China and India will build eight hundred new coal-based electric generation plants by 2012. These new plants will burn nine hundred million tons of coal every year, dumping an additional 2.5 billion tons of carbon dioxide into the atmosphere on an annual basis. According to Zakara, if all of the signers of the Kyoto Accord fully implement their commitments, their actions will reduce their emissions of CO_2 by only 483 million tons, less than 20 percent of the incremental emissions from the new Chinese and Indian coal plants.

If Al Gore were really concerned about global warming, he would be spending most of his time in Beijing and New Delhi working on this problem, not hosting rock concerts or campaigning for the Nobel Peace prize or leading a venture capital group whose profitability depends on selling the global warming theory. If these countries do not change, we are all screwed and we should start building the flood walls around this country's beaches now in anticipation of the global warming impact. Thus, rather than worry about the little stuff (Roger Clemons using steroids, New England

Patriots videotaping opponents, healthy food in the Congressional cafeteria, etc.), the political class should be working on this huge problem. Americans will step up to the plate and help in the global warming fight in their own lives; the political class needs to find a way to the get rest of the world to do the same.

This is a frog in the beaker situation. It is literally getting pretty warm around the world, and unless the political class finds a way to work with China and India on clean coal-based energy and on global warming, it will soon be too hot to get humanity out of the beaker to safety.

Too bad all of the people who really know how to run the country are busy driving cabs and cutting hair.

—George Burns

Social Issues

Step 26

Convene a panel of drug abuse experts from various fields whose purpose will be to completely reexamine the current national drug abuse problem and develop several potential solutions to be reviewed and voted on by the citizens, not Congress or the political class.

The government has been at war against drugs for decades, spending untold billions of dollars and imprisoning untold number of citizens in the process. And the result? Drugs are still readily available to anyone who wants to find them, American civil rights have been abused, and the drug cartels and narco nations continue to prosper. Maybe the "war" tactics need to be changed, because spending and imprisoning do not seem to be working.

However, there are no changes from the political class on the horizon. We send military advisors to Columbia and other nations to help in the "war," but if that has been successful then most of have not heard about the success. And when has putting American troops on foreign soil been a good idea in the past fifty years? The political class has neither the imagination, courage, or initiative to get this situation under control. If they did, the problem would have been resolved long ago.

A likely problem with our "war" strategy has been to concentrate way too much on the supply side of the equation—stopping and confiscating drugs as law enforcement comes across them, rather than reducing the demand for drugs by users. I do not know if this is the answer, but nothing else has worked, so why not try a different equation?

Consider three observations: 1) The political class has shown no desire to reassess and redirect efforts against the plague of drugs. 2) Whenever a difficult issue needs to be addressed, the political class dodges the issues and forms a special panel to investigate and provide recommendations in order to not endanger their re-election (e.g., military base closings, post 9-11 investigation, the Grace Commission from the 1980s, etc.). 3) There are some very smart people throughout this country in medical, law enforcement, economic, sociological, and other fields who could probably come up with a better "war" plan then we currently suffer under. They would bring their own special knowledge to the table and would also make use of experts from overseas who may have different policies, experiences, and laws regarding drug usage and abuse in their countries.

Given these three conditions (nonaction by the political class, the success of past commissions to get things done despite the political class, and the multitude of smart people throughout the country), this problem would be addressed by forming a national panel of experts to address the drug epidemic. This panel would start at ground zero—that is, assume that there is no drug policy in force today and assume that all options are on the table. These options could range from complete legalization of all drugs to the death penalty for possession. Educated, expert panel members could decide on any set of alternative plans that lie between these two extremes.

The proposed solutions would each include a price tag, imple-mentation schedule, milestones, and listing of the pros and cons of each option. The political class would get to nominate and vote on who would be on the panel, but here's the twist: Congress would not decide what plan/strategy would be implemented. The set of alternative plans would be voted on by the citizens of the United States in a national referendum.

Much like that worthless used car, the war on drugs has been an expensive failure on many fronts as waged by the political class. Let's take the problem out of the hands of the political class and put it into the hands of the experts. They certainly cannot do a worse job than has been done and hopefully can start saving the American lives and freedoms lost to addiction. They can bring the latex gloves to the problem and not the oven mitts the political class has used.

What are the politicians going to tell the people when the Constitution is gone and we still have a drug problem?
—William Simpson

Step 27

Make meaningful education reform and improvement a top federal government priority to ensure economic vitality and growth in the future. This will be accomplished by convening an expert panel to make new policy to be approved by the voters, not Congress.

In 1983, during Ronald Reagan's presidency, the National Commission on Excellence in Education was formed to study the effectiveness of education in the United States. According to the Commission: "The education foundations of our society are presently being eroded by a rising tide of mediocrity that threatens our very future as a nation and a people." The Commission's final report proposed numerous changes that would help improve the nation's education system.

Fast-forward to 2006, twenty three years later. Every three years, the Program for International Student Assessment (PISA) conducts an extensive international survey of fifteen-year-old students to assess their abilities in a number of academic fields. The most recent survey in 2006 included students from fifty-seven nations. In science literacy, the United States finished below the overall international average and scored lower than twenty-two other nations. In mathematics literacy, the United States finished below the overall international average and scored lower than thirty-one nations. In both areas, science and mathematics, countries such as Estonia,

Slovenia, Macau, and Liechtenstein finished significantly higher in average scores.

Thus, more than twenty years after the warning from the 1983 National Commission on Excellence in Education, covering times when both the Democrats and Republicans controlled either Congress or the White House, nothing has changed. These embarrassing results occurred despite spending untold billions of taxpayer dollars on education.

Need more proof that the political class does not know how to fix the country's broken education system and processes? Consider the following lead paragraph from a front page article in the *St. Petersburg Times* on April 2, 2008, an article that contained information from the *Washington Post* and Associated Press:

> The $6 billion reading program at the heart of President Bush's No Child Left Behind education law has failed to make a difference in how well children understand what they read, according to a study by the program's own champion, the U.S. Department of Education.

As with the previous national problem, drug addiction, faulty public schooling has been another area where the political class has not come up with any kind of strategic or effective learning plan for the nation's school kids for decades. While a case could be made that the No Child Left Behind law has helped with school and teacher accountability, the flipside argument has been made that the law places too much emphasis on standardized testing and not enough on the learning process, a case made stronger by this latest report showing that reading comprehension has not improved despite throwing six billion dollars at the problem.

Whatever the problem, it is pretty clear that the United States is falling behind in the field of education relative to the rest of the world despite spending incredible amounts of money on public education. I do not have the answers, as I know very little about the educational profession and the education process. However, I am not alone. Based on their ineffective efforts, the political class appears to know just as little as me. The time for them to be entrusted with this important job should come to an end, given their abject failure to keep the United States competitive.

As with the drug problem, a panel would be created under this proposal that included smart educators, economists, sociologists, and others who would develop, price, and plan out a small set of different education plans. These plans would be a ground-up approach, similar to the drug panel's principle, and could range from doing nothing different to completely privatizing all education.

These different plans would then be voted on by all of the citizens and the winning plan implemented. Congress/the political class would appoint and fund the panel, and they would then be out of the picture. Their historic lack of courage, imagination, and initiative in this area disqualifies them from making any meaningful decisions in this area.

Much like that worthless used car, the effort to improve education in this country has been a total failure on many fronts as implemented by the political class. Let's take the problem out of the hands of the political class and put it into the hands of the experts. They certainly cannot do a worse job than has been done, and hopefully can start educating our kids with the tools they will need to survive in a global marketplace. They can bring the latex gloves to the problem and not the oven mitts the political class has used.

Upon the education of the people of this country the fate of this country depends.

—Benjamin Disraeli

Step 28

Convene an expert panel to undertake an in-depth national economic study to determine the real root causes of spiraling health care costs and recommend appropriate actions to eliminate them. Voters, not Congress, will approve these recommendations.

Let's say you have a cough that you want to get treated. You would probably go to your family doctor, who would have to pick from the following list of potential causes:

- you have an allergy
- you have a head cold
- you have the flu
- you have strep throat
- you have bronchitis
- you have pneumonia
- you have lung cancer

Obviously, the course of treatment your doctor recommends will be based on his analysis of the situation using the tools at his disposal, including his expert training, his experience, and his review of your family history. He would not remove a lung before he proved that you had cancer.

Let's expand this example into the broader view of the current state of the American health care system. Our cough is represented by the high cost of health care. Is this high cost the result of:

- obscene profits by doctors, drug companies, insurance companies, hospitals, or all of the above

- incompetence by doctors, drug companies, insurance companies, hospitals, or all of the above

- obscene profits from malpractice suits filed by greedy attorneys

- fraud and theft from insurance companies and government programs

- intrusion of government into the health care business

Like the doctor looking for the cause of the cough, you would hope the political class would first look for the cause of high costs in United States health care and put together a plan to fix the problem, not fix the symptom (high costs). However, nothing could be further from the truth. Presidential candidates in 2008 all touted their health care reform policies, but in none of them did they spell out what is wrong. Do doctors make too much money? Is there too much fraud from both patients and doctors in the system? By not knowing the root causes of high health care costs, there is little hope of finding the right solution to fix that problem.

All of the 2008 presidential candidates' programs called for spending/wasting more and more taxpayer dollars to reduce costs (or decrease coverage because of the high costs) without solving the underlying, unidentified problems. Remember the useless used car vignette. What political-class program actually works, especially one where they do not know what problem they are solving? Their health care reform program would probably call for the removal of a lung to cure strep throat. While the operation may be a success, you still have the cough and significantly less money due to the cost of the operation.

Note: do not ignore the last potential cause of high health-care costs in the country mentioned above, intrusion of government into the health care market. Harry Browne, in his book *Why Government Doesn't Work*, makes a very reasoned, detailed, and viable argument that we would all be better off healthwise if government and the political class got out of the health care business altogether. However, that would require that the political class give up power and influence over Americans and their freedom, something we know will not happen easily.

Thus, a national debate and analysis is needed, by an expert panel that does not include the political class, to analyze the health care market, profitability, government intrusion, fraud, etc., and formulate a national referendum to be voted on by Americans, not Congress, on how to solve the problem.

Much like that worthless used car, the problem of health care in this country has been around for a long time, and not addressed successfully for just as long by the political class. Let's take the problem out of the hands of the political class and let the experts give it a try. They certainly cannot do a worse job than has been done and hopefully can start saving the American lives and freedoms lost to health care issues. They can bring the latex gloves to the problem, and not the oven mitts the political class has used.

Our major obligation is not to mistake slogans for solutions.

—Edward R. Murrow

Step 29

Make total immigration reform and improvement a top government priority to ensure economic vitality and growth in the future. This will be accomplished by convening an expert panel to make new policy to be approved by the voters, not Congress.

As with drug addiction, education problems, and rising medical costs, the political class has accomplished virtually nothing in the area of immigration policy and reform. While estimates vary significantly, most sources involved with immigration would agree that there are at least ten million illegal aliens currently within the boundaries of the United States.

Depending on what side of the political class you reside in, these illegal immigrants are either contributing to the good of society by performing jobs that current citizens would not undertake, which helps hold down prices in the food and tourism industries, or they are lawbreaking parasites that use up tax dollars from current citizens in the form of border patrols, social services, and criminal activities. The debate always gets emotional and nothing ever gets done. No comprehensive, commonsense policy is formed or executed, and the same old border cat and mouse games go on forever.

One proposed but extreme remedy is to round up these millions of illegal immigrants and send them back home. There are a few problems with this. First, given the inability of the political class to do anything effectively and efficiently, do we really believe that this government has the ability to find, apprehend, and deport over ten million people, many of whom are living secretly through-out the country? Even if they could be found, what would be the cost of the roundup in both dollars and resources better spent on other issues? What would be the economic impact to the rest of us if crops are not harvested, tourism needs not serviced, and other jobs not fulfilled? Finally, from the perspective of freedom, do we really want federal agents sweeping through our communities?

Conversely, do we really want our borders to be so wide open that all types of people from other countries can stroll right in? A country that cannot control its borders is a country that may not be able to control its fate, as any immigrant could be a criminal, a terrorist, or an honest worker. Are the law enforcement, social services, and educational resources that are used up by immigrants worth the financial benefit that they may create?

For every immigrant who drains our resources, there are many others who have recently made incredible contributions to the vi-tality and business of America:

- Sergey Brin: born in Russia and the cofounder of Google

- Andrew Grove: born in Hungary and the cofounder of Intel

- Kevoak Hovnanian: born in Iraq and cofounder of national builder Hovanian Enterprises

- Liz Clairborne: born in Belgium and founder of her own ap-parel company

- Jerry Yang: born in China and cofounder of Yahoo!

- William Mow: born in China and founder of Bugle Boy ap-parel

- Charles Wang: born in China and founder of Computer Associates

- Andreas Von Bechtolsheim and Vinod Khosla: born in Germany and Russia, respectively, and cofounders of Sun Microsystems

As you can see, the debate is wide ranging and difficult, with pros and cons on both sides. Given the situation, trusting the political class to come up with a workable remedy is fruitless. Thus, as with the other major social problems, an expert panel would be created under this proposal that included law enforcement, economists, sociologists, and others who would develop, price, and plan out a small set of different immigration plans. These plans would be a ground-up approach, and could range from doing nothing different to completely walling off our borders to opening up our borders to anyone at anytime.

These different plans would then be voted on by all of the citizens and the winning plan implemented. Congress/the political class would appoint and fund the panel, and they would then be out of the picture. Their historic lack of courage, imagination, and initiative in this area disqualifies them from making any meaningful decisions in this vital issue going forward.

Much like that worthless used car, the effort to craft a wise and prudent immigration policy for the country has been a total failure on many fronts as implemented by the political class. Let's take the problem out of the hands of the political class and put it into the hands of the experts. They certainly cannot do a worse job than has been done and hopefully can help us understand the true tradeoffs, downsides, and benefits of a comprehensive immigration plan. They can bring latex gloves to the problem, and not the oven mitts the political class has used.

An injustice anywhere threatens justice everywhere.
—Martin Luther King

Foreign Policy

Step 30

Bring back all nonessential deployed military personnel back to the United States. This will save money and help improve our reputation as a freedom loving, non-imperialistic nation.

Although we try not to be hated as a nation, it seems that it is harder and harder not to be resented by the rest of the world. American prestige, for any number of reasons, has steadily decreased over the past twenty years as our military and political presence and interference in world affairs has increased. Could there be a correlation between our increased meddling and the decrease in respect?

One of the reasons that Bin Laden claimed he attacked the United States was that we had stationed troops in his homeland of Saudi Arabia. His attack resulted in more troops being stationed in the Middle East and further resentment. One of the problems we have with North Korea is the stationing of almost thirty thousand American troops on the Korean peninsula over fifty years after the war ended. Every year or so we hear about a GI being accused of rape on Okinawa where we have 25,000 troops stationed. The stories go on and on, and the stationing of troops overseas gets the United States bad news coverage and public relations with little positive benefits in return.

Thus, a fundamental foreign question needs to be addressed: given the bad news and the costs that foreign stationing of troops causes, why do we continue to do it? South Korea currently has almost seven hundred thousand people serving in its armed forces. If

North Korea decides to attack South Korea with its one million man army, thirty thousand United States troops are not going to make a difference in the outcome. Do we still think that Japan is such a national menace that we need to station twenty-five thousand troops there? If Japan is really not the menace, do we have twenty-five thousand troops there to keep China in line? Let's be honest: if China decided to come across and take over Taiwan, twenty-five thousand United States troops in Japan would make no difference.

South Korea has about the twelfth largest economy in the world; it should be using its own resources and money to defend itself, not the U.S. taxpayers' money. Given that the twenty-five thousand troops in Japan serve no deterrence purpose, they should also be redeployed back to this country, saving money and avoiding bad press.

Why do we have any military presence in Europe? Are we afraid the World War II Axis powers will come back to life, or that Russia (not the Soviet Union, which no longer exists) will come over the Iron Curtain (oops, that no longer exists either)? We have to realize as a nation that stationing U.S. troops in sufficient quantities to be a deterrence is no longer possible or economically a wise thing to do.

Thus, nonessential deployments of U.S. forces in South Korea, Japan, the Philippines, Columbia, and elsewhere should be immediately scaled back, if not eliminated completely. Deploying U.S. troops in just Japan and Korea alone costs billions of dollars each year with no strategic or defensive gain in return.

This action is a freedom pyramid issue. Very seldom does U.S. intervention in a foreign country promote the American ideal of freedom. Rather, it has usually resulted in resentment toward the U.S. and a costly waste of money for American taxpayers.

Those who refuse to learn from history are condemned to repeat it.

—George Santayana

Step 31

Close the Guantanamo Bay prison facility as soon as possible after the remaining prisoners have their day in court to determine innocence or guilt.

The attacks on September 11, 2001, were among the most traumatic events to ever hit this country. The loss of life, property, and sense of security were overwhelming. It is no surprise that the United States responded promptly and aggressively to root out and track down those responsible. Putting those captured early in the war into hastily assembled prison compounds at Guantanamo Bay was a stroke of genius because it nullified any attempt by their cohorts to break them out and, in the process, endanger additional American lives.

However, seven years after their capture, those sent there have not had their day in court, a basic premise of American freedom and justice. The government missed an incredible opportunity to show the world that although we suffered serious losses in the attacks, we were not abandoning a basic premise of our society, the right to a speedy, and fair trial. In light of this behavior—our lack of concern for justice for those in our prison at Guantanamo—our claims to being a fair and just, liberty-loving society ring a little hollow around the world. If these prisoners had been tried quickly and their status, either guilty or innocent, had been taken care of years ago, it would have struck a chord of respect for the country from around the world.

However, this is not the case, and the U.S. government comes off as the big bully on the block. We ended up imprisoning the lowest level of terrorists and then denied them justice and/or redemption. Thus, expedited but fair trial proceedings should be instituted to determine the status of these prisoners, freeing them or sending them to conventional prisons and shutting down the facility as soon as possible, removing a bad public relations stain from the country.

Note: President Obama has signed an executive order in early 2009 to close this facility sometime in the future. However, since this facility has not been closed as of the publication of this book, it will remain as an important step that still needs to be taken to help restore the American concept of freedom and fairness.

You cannot believe in the freedom pyramid or convince the world that you do if you insist on holding people for an indeterminate amount of time without providing them a day in court, regardless of how they came into your possession. By not exhibiting this degree of justice to those at Guantanamo, America cannot claim the high road in any facet of world affairs. Most importantly, by denying the internees any rights, the political class will find it a little easier to extend that denial of rights to American citizens in the future.

The greatest crime since World War II has been U.S. foreign policy.

—Ramsey Clark

Step 32

End the Cuban trade embargo immediately.
After almost fifty years it has not been effective
in removing Castro from power, it denies U.S.
companies a convenient marketplace, it separates
family members from each other, and it diminishes
the ability of the Cuban people to live in a
democracy.

What do the following presidents have in common:

Kennedy

Johnson

Nixon

Carter

Reagan

Bush I

Clinton

In total, they were all in power in America less time than Fidel Castro was in power in Cuba, even though any number of initiatives were instituted by the above presidents to remove Castro from power. After more than forty years of boycotting a nation just ninety miles from our coast, and showing nothing for our efforts, one would think that a change in strategy might be warranted. Given that the boycott has been an abysmal failure, maybe dialog, trade, and exposing the Cuban people to the concepts of freedom, liberty, and open markets would have been more successful in getting rid of Castro.

However, from a political class perspective, getting rid of Castro would not have been beneficial. Castro has been used by any number of presidents and presidential contenders to rally support for their campaigns and terms by energizing those who want to get rid of Castro. By talking tough, they have a constant issue to hopefully garner votes by keeping the status quo intact. Even though the status quo has proven ineffective for almost fifty years, any policy, no matter how bad in reality and from a logical perspective, is good in the political sense if it gets votes.

This boycott stance flies in the face of freedom, something that America should stand for. As with the Guantanamo Bay prisoners, we come off not as a liberty-loving country but as the big bullies on the block. Castro and Cuba are no longer military threats, and thus this boycott should be stopped immediately. It removes another stigma to our long-running but ineffective foreign policy, opens up a new, nearby trading partner, exposes the Cuban people to new and hopefully freedom-inducing experiences. It also removes another freedom-stifling opportunity for the American political class.

The Freedom Pyramid should extend to all the world's people and not be denied by the United States or the political class.

The definition of stupidity is doing the same thing over and over again and expecting different results.
—Albert Einstein

Political Behavior

Step 33

Prohibit non-government entities from paying
for any fact-finding mission for any president,
U.S. senator, or congressman/woman or their
staffs. Certain geographic areas should be off-
limits for fact-finding missions unless ultra-special
circumstances can be justified. These off-limit areas
include Hawaii, Florida, and California coasts, the
Bahamas, Tahiti, any attractive foreign locale, and
any golf, ski, or tennis resort.

Consider excerpts from a Knight Ridder newspaper article in early 2008 that highlighted findings from the Center for Public Integrity:

- Private groups, corporations, or trade associations—many with legislation that could affect them pending in Congress—paid nearly $50 million since 2000 to send members of Congress and their staffers on at least twenty-three thousand trips.

- These trips included at least two hundred trips to Paris, France, and also included at least 150 trips to Hawaii.

- Some of these trips included $500-a-night hotel stays, and some included the use of corporate jets that cost up to $25 thousand a trip.

- Twenty-five members of Congress received more than $120 thousand each in free travel.

This change is pretty straightforward. As an elected official, you would not be allowed to go anywhere that is either paid for by a non-government entity or go anywhere that is "nice." The first part of the requirement would attempt to keep the political class member unaffected and unswayed by the money that the non-government entity (union, corporation, lobbyist, foreign country) was paying out for the trip. While traveling on the taxpayers' money may be more expensive in the short-term, it would help avoid future wasteful government spending programs that occur as a result of a paid trip. Under no circumstance could you take a family member or friend along on the trip unless they paid for themselves.

Certain geographic areas would be off limits in almost all situations. For example, a congressman from Indiana would not be allowed to travel to Hawaii for any reason except on his own vacation using his own money. Hawaii, the Caribbean, resorts, London, Paris, Rome, etc., would also be off-limits. To help insure that this restriction was being complied with, all elected officials would be required to disclose their travel plans to their constituents prior to traveling if the trip was outside their district or state. The only exceptions would be if they were traveling to those countries that are on the State Department's restricted list (i.e., the danger spots around the globe). However, they would have to report their travels to these locations after they returned.

This is another "let them eat cake" example, where the political class gets to go to exotic locations under the guise of governing while ordinary Americans struggle to pay their bills and mortgages, and maybe treat themselves to some sort of limited vacation.

I either want less corruption, or more chance to participate in it.

—Ashleigh Brilliant

Step 34

Hold Congress and Senate committees and subcommittees accountable for their respective areas of responsibility, and remove committee members from committee posts if they do not meet minimal performance criteria.

Theoretically, our congressional system is run by a series of committees and subcommittees of elected officials that meet on a regular basis to gather and analyze information and propose laws that will improve the country and its citizens. In fact, that is their major role: to be informed and use that knowledge to move the country forward. They are like a company's board of directors, guiding the actions of government agencies/business units based on an overarching perspective.

However, given the current state of the government, a case can be made that they have not been doing a very good job. And more than that, there is no accountability for their actions or lack of action. A few examples:

- Everyone would agree that the 9-11 attacks represented a system wide failure in U.S. intelligence, a failure that ranged from FBI and CIA analysts to current and past presidents *and* … the congressional intelligence committees that should have overseen and guided the entire operation. If a company fails to be successful, much of the blame usually falls on both the executives of that company and the board of directors who failed to give meaningful direction. The 9-11 disaster cost American lives, and the political class, be it the presidents or the congressional intelligence committees involved, was an absolute failure.

- According to Mapquest, it is less than eight miles from the Capitol building to Walter Reed Hospital, one of the main federal hospitals serving the wounded soldiers from Iraq. However, in 2006 a major crisis came to light revealing the deplorable medical conditions that these returning heroes were subjected to at Walter Reed and other military medical facilities. Apparently the Senate and House committees responsible for overseeing this and other facilities like it did not even have enough energy, interest, or dedication to take the eight-mile trip to see how poorly their committees were serving our servicemen and women.

- Several years ago it was reported that the Department of Agriculture could not account for $5 billion in its books. $5 billion in single dollar bills laid end to end would stretch around the world almost four times, but the Department of Agriculture and the Congressional committees that oversaw the Department lost it. There were apparently no ramifications for the loss. In fact, to add insult to injury, the Department of Agriculture asked Congress for $100 million to investigate how and where they lost the $5 billion in the first place (BNET Business Management, November 20, 2000).

The list could go on and on. Congressional oversight and leadership is nonexistent or, in the case of 9-11, fatal to American citizens. However, despite this lousy performance record, the political class members who serve on these committees are not held accountable for their actions. After 9-11, all of the current members of both the House and Senate intelligence committees should have been replaced for incompetence. It happens in the real word outside of DC—either perform your job up to established performance criteria or be fired. It should also happen to the political class. Subject wounded soldiers to horrific conditions, and you should be replaced. Lose $5 billion of taxpayer money, and you should be replaced.

Now the defenders of these poorly performing committees would say that those in Congress serving on these committees are the best people available and should continue to serve. Even though the intelligence committees failed the country on 9-11 in not providing adequate protection, they did as a good a job as anyone else serving in Congress at that time. This argument is faulty in that it rewards incompetence: although we are incompetent, others would have been more incompetent. I do not think the three thousand Americans who died that day would take much solace in that argument.

How would we decide when members of a committee should be removed for incompetence? Two approaches could be easily implemented:

- A national survey would be conducted every year that would ask a cross section of Americans whether they thought any part of Congress (i.e., any Congressional committee) was not performing up to acceptable levels. If they did not attain minimal satisfaction ratings, then those members would be immediately replaced on the committee.

- A second approach would add a single page to every taxpayer's 1040 tax return. They would be able to check off which parts of government are severely under performing.

Conversely, either the national survey or the 1040 tax return could ask about those committees that are performing above and beyond expectations. This would result in recognition and possibly monetary rewards for doing a better-than-average job. Whatever approach is used, some way must be found to push accountability onto the political class—accountability that does not exist today.

This is just another "let them eat cake" example from the political class. They got elected, so accountability to anyone is a thing of the past. Because they control all of the election processes, their incompetence is not a problem from their point of view.

> **Suppose you were an idiot and suppose you were a member of Congress ... But I repeat myself.**
>
> —*Mark Twain*

Step 35

Make any proven improper sexual relations with a
government intern, page, or government employee
immediate grounds for dismissal from national
political office and a lifelong ban on running for
any elected political office or appointment to any
government position or lobbyist job.

onsider the known track record of recent political class misdoings:

- A married, two-term president is sexually serviced by a
  young female intern.

- A longtime advocate for children allegedly turns out to be a
  sexual predator on congressional pages.

- A longtime senator allegedly patrols public restrooms for
  sexual encounters.

- A married, longtime California congressman allegedly has
  an affair with a young female intern, who shortly afterwards
  is found dead.

- A married New York governor allegedly utilizes a high-
  priced call girl operation in a high-profile DC hotel.

Now, someone might say that these affairs are private matters and should not be judged by anyone but those involved.
Unfortunately, these are not private matters when they are done

by public figures. Affairs of this type take up tremendous time and effort, two traits that would be better spent fixing the country's ills. Is it not possible that if Clinton spent less time with Monica and the ramifications that arose from her, and more time on national security, that 9-11 may have been averted? Just a thought. If the Republicans had not been so preoccupied with Monica and Bill, might they have had more time to spend on national security and helped avert the 9-11 attacks? Just a thought. If Congressman Mark Foley had spent more time on legislative issues and less on allegedly chasing pages, might he have made a bigger contribution to helping the country? Just a thought.

I do not know what the answer is, but some sort of code of conduct, one that has teeth and is enforceable, needs to be established to keep public figures focused on public issues while in office.

This is a variation on the five-legged-dog syndrome; just because we may think of some past politicians as being noble and statesmanlike (e.g., Jefferson, Roosevelt, Lincoln, Washington) does not mean that all politicians are noble.

If we ever pass out as a great nation we ought to put on our tombstone, "America died from a delusion that she has moral leadership."

—*Will Rogers*

Step 36

Require all members of the political class, upon election to Congress or the White House, to take and pass a course on economic theory and principles. This will help them better understand how their actions will impact the lives of Americans, both short-term and long-term.

Most times politicians act not in the best interest of the country, but in the best interest of their image or reelection hopes. Whether this is done through ignorance or arrogance, the financial and economic impacts of their actions often go far beyond the immediate issues they are addressing. Consider the following basic economic supply and demand examples that Congress has ignored:

- In their haste to wean America off of foreign oil, the political class recently passed legislation that encourages (i.e., bribes) Iowa farmers and the like to divert their corn crops from their current uses into the making of ethanol, which will be blended with oil to reduce dependency on foreign oil sources. However, did any member of the political class stop to ask what might happen to food prices when the supply of corn is reduced in the food supply chain and moved into the energy supply chain? Simple economic theory says that when supply goes down, prices go up. Thus, in their rush to fix one national problem, energy dependence, they contributed to another national problem, inflation. Corn is used in a wide variety of foodstuffs as well as being used for cattle feed. Drive up the price of corn and the price of many other items go up.

Now you might say that the price increase in the food chain is worth a little less dependency on foreign oil. However, there are two weaknesses in this argument:

1) Corn is probably one of the less efficient crops to use for the production of ethanol. Encouraging the research and development of other ethanol sources would have reduced oil dependency while not affecting the food chain price stream. However, this would not have allowed the political class to march into the Iowa presidential primary caucuses with free corn farmer money to influence the primary results.

2) An inexpensive source of ethanol is already available, namely ethanol brewed from sugar crops in South America. It is plentiful and cheap, but Congress currently slaps a hefty tariff on its importation. Removing the tariff would immediately create a flow of cheap ethanol and help reduce our oil dependency without affecting the food chain. While we would still have dependency on a foreign energy source, it would in theory be a friendlier source from a political perspective, it would diversify our energy suppliers, and would buy us time to get our own ethanol production efficiently underway.

• A second example is the current state of the U.S. dollar versus other currencies. In a word, it stinks. One of the main contributing factors to the fall of the dollar is that the political class continues to issue more and more bonds to cover the cost of its excessive and wasteful spending. Simple economics: the more there is of some-

thing in the market, the less valuable each thing is (supply and demand from Economics 101).

It can only be hoped that some kind of economic training would
help improve the quality of their decision making and add some
discipline to their spending, and misspending, of taxpayer dollars.

This is another example of the useless used car. Nothing works
in this country, and many times it is because the ruling political
class does not understand basic economics or decides to ignore the
rules of basic economics. In either case, the car (the country) continues to break down because the mechanics (the politicians) do not
understand how things work.

**The first lesson of economics is scarcity. There is never
enough of anything to satisfy all those who want it. The
first lesson of politics is to disregard the first lesson of
economics.**

—Thomas Sowell

Step 37

Base pay increases for congressional members on an annual customer satisfaction rating, and repeal the current practice of automatically increasing congressional pay without a vote.

Every year the political class rewards its elected members with an automatic 2 to 3 percent pay increase (source: www.senate.gov) regardless of their performance or how well or badly the country is doing. This pay raise does not require any debate or voting; the political class has rigged it to automatically occur with a minimal amount of public attention—a very sweet arrangement.

How great would it be if your job worked that way? Automatic pay raises regardless of how well you did your job, regardless of whether you came to work or not, regardless of how hard you worked if and when you were at work, etc. Again, as mentioned previously, there is not accountability for the political class. Thus, the proposed change here is that this automatic pay increase process be scrapped immediately and pay raises be based on performance.

The process for evaluating performance could be quite simple. A national, statistically balanced year-end survey would ask Americans how well their government is functioning in total. It would not be specific to a state's congressional delegation. The purpose is to have the whole country do better, not measure how well the home state political class brings home the pork. Pay raises and pay cuts would be based on the outcome of the survey.

A second, alternative approach would be to put it on the ballot for the congressional elections every two years. Vote for your congressman or woman, vote for your choice for senator, and vote on how well the last two years went for the country, with your opinion determining how well or poorly the political class should be paid.

By focusing the measurement process on how well the whole country is doing, it would hopefully force the two major political parties to play nice together for the benefit of all. Just serving your particular voting bloc while alienating other United States citizens would not be enough to get good marks for performance.

Let them eat cake: "We have been elected, and thus we must be important enough and smart enough to determine how to pay ourselves."

"Did you ever notice that when you put the words "The" and "IRS" together, it spells THEIRS?

—*Author Unknown*

Step 38

Require all congressional members, the president, and vice president to annually sign off on a "shared values" statement. This statement would guide their behavior and interactions in order to create a political atmosphere more conducive to progress and freedom.

Many American businesses realized long ago that the productivity of their employees would improve dramatically if the business could develop and communicate a set of values that they wanted their employees to live by. Having a set of shared values that guided how the business operated allowed for better teamwork, improved focus on important goals and objectives, and helped employees understand how to productively behave when confronted with a problem. Although this concept may seem hokey to many who never experienced a shared-values environment, the notion of commonality of behavior and values has been proven and accepted in many workplaces.

Now think about this concept and how it does not apply to the political class today. Remember back a few years ago when Vice President Cheney and Senator Leahy of Vermont exchanged f-bombs on the floor of the Senate. Think about the venom and misinformation that the political class spread about their opponents during elections. Hardly an environment of cooperation and compromise for the benefit of all. Thus, it is time that the political class be held to a high standard of shared values, a prototype that might have the following components:

- *Respect:* to show consideration for, to avoid violation of, to treat with deference

- *Trust:* firm reliance on the ability or character of a person or thing, a confident belief

- *Commitment:* to pledge to do something

- *Innovation:* to begin or introduce something new, creative

- *Integrity:* adherence to a code of honest behavior

- *Quality:* excellence, superiority

- *Teamwork:* cooperative effort by members of a team to achieve a common goal

Compare these ideals to today's reality:

- *Respect:* given current political muckraking and dirty tricks, there is very little respect between politicians and by politicians for those who may oppose their election.

- *Trust:* the political class makes sure that American "tribes" do not trust each other in order to get themselves reelected over and over again. In fact, they rely on and propagate mistrust to energize their base.

- *Commitment:* their commitment is only to their reelection, undertaking no serious or difficult position to further the short-term or long-term good of the country because that may endanger their reelection potential.

- *Innovation:* as stated earlier in this book, nothing that the political class touches works, whether it is FEMA in New Orleans, faulty roads in Massachusetts and Minnesota, a non-existent energy plan, etc. Innovation beyond getting elected does not exist in the mind of the political class.

- *Integrity:* Hillary Clinton's fabrication that she came under sniper fire in Bosnia says it all about a politician's integrity.

- *Quality:* see innovation above.

- *Teamwork:* nonexistent.

Two things would have to happen for this change to take hold:

1. Political leaders would have to demonstrate and live these behaviors at all times and in all situations.

2. Their behavior would have to be measured and the results used to reward or punish behavior relative to the shared values proposition. This measurement would be a component of the annual assessment outlined in the previous change.

Think about how much better the country would be if the political class would act more civilly toward each other and toward individual citizens using a shared values approach in the overall context of freedom. It certainly cannot hurt to have a set of moral behavior standards for politicians; having none for the past few decades has not worked.

The frog in the beaker: we as a country and government have slowly gotten away from the principles and morals that made this country unique (respect, integrity, innovation, etc.), and the water is getting hotter and hotter as we allow these principles to further erode, an erosion that has been led by the current crop of the political class.

My creed is that public service must be more than doing a job efficiently and honestly. It must be a complete dedication to the people and to the nation with full recognition that every human being is entitled to courtesy and consideration, that constructive criticism is not only to be expected but sought, that smears are not only to be expected but fought, that honor is to be earned, not bought.

—Margaret Chase Smith

Step 39

Restrict all United States senators to one six-year term, and all members of the United States House of Representatives to either one four-year term or two two-year terms.

Think back to 1959:

- Microwave ovens did not exist.

- Cell phones were still just a dream.

- Personal computers were not even a dream.

- Beetles were just small bugs or cars, not a rock and roll legend.

- The U.S. population was 178 million, about 40 percent less than it is today.

- Communism was the number one foreign affairs issue.

- Gasoline cost about twenty-five cents a gallon, and the average home cost about $12,400.

- Honda made small motorcycles … and what is a Toyota?

- And, while we are at it, what is a Kurd, a Shiite, or a Sunni?

The world has changed a lot since 1959, the year that Senator Robert Byrd was first elected to the Senate. While not as famous, others from the political class have occupied congressional seats for years or decades. And maybe that is the problem the country faces. Without term limits, we end up with the same tired members of the political class being elected over and over again, many of whom came from a different world originally, a world that does not exist anymore.

It is finally time to try something new and implement term limits as soon as possible in order to enable a fresh look at what ails this country instead of relying on the same people who got us into the problems we face. If you are not part of the solution (which the political class is not based on its track record), then you must be part of the problem. If the president, the most important political figure in the world, is restricted to no more than eight years in that office, why should less important people such as congressmen and senators be allowed to serve longer than the president? By not giving them term limits, are we saying that they are more critical to the country than the president?

Thus, from now on, a senator gets one six-year term and a congressman or woman gets no more than four years. They are then out and new people and new ideas come in. By restricting the length of service, elected representatives might actually do something noble and courageous for once, since they have a limited amount of time to make a bold, positive impact and they are not beholden to anyone for reelection. They might do the right thing for the country and not for themselves.

Useless used car: If anyone should be blamed for government failures over the past thirty years, it should be those members of the political class who are not part of the solution, and thus part of the problem. We need to get these useless used cars out of Washington, as they have proven over the decades that they cannot solve anything.

The government is merely a servant—merely a temporary servant; it cannot be its prerogative to determine what is right and what is wrong, and decide who is a patriot and who isn't. Its function is to obey orders, not originate them.

—Mark Twain

Step 40

Prohibit ex-senators, ex-congressmen, or ex-presidents from registering with, working for, or getting any benefit from any lobbying organization for ten years after they leave office.

Recently, **Trent Lott, a longtime** Republican senator from Mississippi, resigned from the Senate in the middle of his term to work for a lobbyist. He probably figured he could make more money lobbying than continuing to have a high-profile Senate position. He resigned prior to new, tighter guidelines that were implemented regarding working for lobbyists. One of the semi-noble attempts to clean up government was about to take effect.

However, rather than semi-noble, let's change it to be truly noble: no working for a registered lobbying organization or business for ten years after your last day in office. Plus, for ten years after you are hired by a lobbying group, you will never be allowed to meet or interact directly with any elected official. All of your work for the lobbying group will have to be in the background, supporting the lobby, not out lobbying your friends and fellow members of the political class.

A Jabba the Hutt example: after gorging themselves on public taxpayer money and perks while in office, the political class goes off and gets more taxpayer money, but through a front organization known as a lobbyist.

If you can't drink a lobbyist's whiskey, take his money, sleep with his wife, and still vote against him in the morning, you don't belong in politics.

—author unknown

Step 41

Prohibit any senator, president, or congressman
whose net worth, not income, is over $3 million
from drawing a paycheck during their term of office,
for the good of the country.

Growing up in America in the 1950s and early 1960s, I was led to believe that there were not many more noble jobs then serving your country. That people ran for office because they wanted to make a positive difference, not because they wanted to make a career out of it and set themselves up for life from the perspective of a pension, prestige, and medical coverage. Given the current federal budget deficit and the struggling of everyday Americans, it makes no sense for the many multimillionaire members of Congress to draw paychecks when the country is in such need. Although the exact numbers are difficult to pin down, given the wide reporting categories by which the political class reports their wealth, consider the following estimates:

- CNN.com reported on June 13, 2003, that at least forty senators were millionaires.

- Forbes reported on November 11, 2006, that about fifty senators were millionaires.

- The Center for Responsive Politics reported that the average net worth of a senator was $8.9 million.

- The website informationclearinghouse.com estimated in 2005 that 28 percent of the members of the House of Representatives were millionaires.

Thus, according to these varied sources, over 30 percent of congressional members are millionaires, while just 1 percent of the country are millionaires.

If serving your country is the main reason to run, then serving your country should be the main reason for forgoing your annual congressional salary. If you have assets worth $3 million and get a conservative, safe 5 percent return on those assets, you will be earning $150 thousand a year by doing nothing, putting you in the top 5 to 6 percent of the nation's earners (Source: U.S. Census Bureau, 2005). Most Americans could live on that amount of money quite easily, and so should the political class.

While it would not balance the budget, having multimillionaire political class members forgo their salaries would be a huge symbolic gesture that we are all in this together and we all need to make sacrifices. If you have less than $3 million in assets, then you would continue to draw a congressional paycheck because you may actually need it to serve.

The Jabba the Hutt syndrome can also pertain to individual members of government, and not just the overall waste that government creates. Given the dire straits the country is in, this symbolic gesture from the many millionaires in Congress would go far in uniting the country for the sacrifices that are needed.

Politics would be a helluva good business if it weren't for the [expletive deleted] people.

—*Richard Nixon*

Step 42

Require ex-presidents whose net income is over $1 million per year to pay back one dollar for every two dollars earned over that amount to help fund their Secret Service protection. Also, require them to forgo their annual pension once their income exceeds $3 million a year or their net assets exceed $10 million.

Legend has it that when Harry Truman's presidential career ended, he boarded a train and returned home to Missouri, not because he enjoyed train rides but because he was not affluent enough to fly home. Once home, he lived off of his small Army pension and his savings since there were no Presidential pensions at that time. Most presidents throughout history did not become rich as a result of serving their country; service was its own reward.

That has changed dramatically over the past twenty years. Many ex-presidents and ex-politicians now earn much more money after serving than when they were in office. Jimmy Carter, George Bush I, and Bill Clinton stayed very active after their terms were over, doing both humanitarian/charity work and making a lot of money giving speeches, sitting on boards. Consider Bill and Hillary Clinton's excellent adventure in capitalism over the past eight years (published in the *St. Petersburg Times* on April 5, 2008):

- Since Bill left office, the Clintons have earned $109 million in eight years.

- Bill himself earned $20,700,000 in 2007 alone.

- Bill's two books have earned him almost $30 million.

- Hillary's last book earned her $20,400,000.

- Bill has earned over $50 million from the lecture/speech circuit.

Do the Clintons still need to accept his annual government pension check of approximately $160,000, less than 1 percent of his 2007 earnings? If he is making it big in the private sector, does the American taxpayer need to continue to subsidize his security needs with government/Secret Service resources?

This change would make Clinton and others like him who can afford Secret Service protection to pay for it themselves. Once their income exceeded the $1 million threshold, they would have to start helping pay for their own security. This would not be a hardship, as earning $1 million a year would put an ex-politician in the upper 1 percent bracket of American workers. It's only fair that once they go beyond the $1 million level that they should start pulling their own weight.

Would this change balance the budget or create a massive tax break for the typical American taxpayer? No, but it would symbolically demonstrate that at least some members of the political class were pulling their own weight, and in the process making a small but symbolic contribution to the country.

This is Jabba the Hutt relative to millionaire politicians. They need more and more without considering how others in the nation are hurting.

Do the right thing. It will gratify some people and astonish the rest of us."

—*Mark Twain*

Step 43

Eliminate the senator-only elevator.

n the Senate wing of the Capitol building is a special elevator. Special in that only members of the U.S. Senate are allowed to ride on it. Given its special status, one would hope it is a special elevator:

- Maybe it makes its occupants smarter. No, not based on the performance of the Senate over the years.

- Maybe they use it for special meetings. No, their offices would be far more comfortable and less vulnerable to security leaks than using a dedicated elevator.

- Maybe it makes them better looking. No, they look the same when they get on as when they get off.

Apparently the only reason for a senator-only elevator is to increase, in a very hollow way, the prestige the Senate bestows on itself. Kind of like the old playground taunt: "Nyah, nyah, nyah, we have something that you don't have!"

Obviously, eliminating the senator-only elevator would have virtually no financial, political, or freedom-inducing impact on the country and its citizens. And there are far more important changes to work on. However, from a symbolic perspective, it would demonstrate that we are all in this together, and that just because one is a senator does not mean that they are much different from every other United States citizen. In times of trouble, symbolism can be very important. It would help offset the elitist view that Senator John Edwards demonstrated in early 2007 when it came to light that he paid $400 for a haircut.

This is just another let them eat cake example where the political class needs to reassure itself that it is special and more important than other U.S. citizens.

Democracy is when the indigent, and not the men of property, are the rulers.

—Aristotle

Step 44

Prohibit the use of federal programs or tax dollars for any project unless it materially benefits a high percentage of residents of at least five states.

onsider the following budget items that have found their way into recent federal budgets:

- $250,000 to connect two ski resorts in New York so that they can compete better with ski resorts in Vermont and New Hampshire.

- $250,000 to Washington State University and Michigan State University for research to cut asparagus industry labor costs.

- $200,000 to Ocean Spray to market white cranberry juice in Great Britain.

- $70,000 to the Paper Industry International Hall of Fame for construction and renovation.

- $300,000 for a feasibility study for the world's first fully enclosed motor speedway.

- $775,000 to the Biltmore Hotel in Coral Gables, Florida, part of a project to provide economic opportunity in areas of low and moderate income (even though the per capita income level in Coral Gables is almost 20 percent above the national average).

- $77,826 for the study "Coping with Change in Czechoslovakia."

- $400,000 to study "The Expressive Culture of the San Blas Islands" in Panama.

- $90,000 to study the social life—not the diet or health—of vegetarians

- And on and on and on.

See Appendix A, Political Class Insanity, to see how this wasted money could be used for more positive purposes.

And according to a May 22, 2007 Los Angeles Times article, published in the St. Petersburg Times, the amount of programs like these have tripled over the past ten years to more than thirteen thousand individual earmarks as the political class uses them to reward donors to their campaigns and demonstrate how well they can rip off other states' taxpayers to the benefit of their own constituents. The political class has shown no remorse or control in eliminating these wasteful programs while other federal programs such as Medicare and Social Security, along with other, more important needs of the country, go untreated and into crisis.

Thus, this change would provide a very simple guideline for these types of programs. Since these are federal taxpayer dollars in play, they should not be used on any individual program unless it clearly benefits the lives of citizens in at least five states. If New York wants to compete with other states in the skiing industry, they should use their own state taxes/money, and not take taxes that citizens in Vermont and New Hampshire paid to use those same dollars against them. If Ocean Spray wants to compete in Great Britain, let them use their own money. Increasing white cranberry usage overseas will not benefit citizens in at least five states.

Two things are needed to make this change happen. First, a president must be elected who is dedicated to stamping out these types of wasteful programs. He or she would have to train Congress to understand that he or she would veto any piece of legislation that contained pork barrel programs even if the overall legislation was worthwhile. Many of these types of programs are inserted into unrelated bills and ride the wave into creation based on the importance of the larger bill being enacted. The president would probably have to veto any number of bills before the message got though: no more state, industry, or individual-specific spending programs. Unfortunately, this would require incredible political strength and fortitude, two assets that are usually found lacking in the political class.

The second need is an understanding from the entire electorate that special interests should not be sucking valuable tax resources into local, unbeneficial uses. By eliminating these parochial uses of our tax dollars, we increase the possibility of holding onto these tax dollars and increasing our own individual freedom.

This is a five-legged-dog example: calling a pork program an earmark does not mean it is not pork and wasteful. By cutting out the pork that the political class generates for its own benefit, the economic freedom that would pass back to Americans would dramatically increase the freedom to run their lives as they see fit using the wealth they create from their own efforts.

There are always too many Democratic congressmen, too many Republican congressmen, and never enough U.S. congressmen."

—author unknown

Step 45

Hold the political class accountable to the same laws, regulations, penalties, fines, and principles required by the rest of America as it pertains to sex/race affirmative action quotas and behavior.

The following table contains information that profiles the sex and race breakdown of Congress:

	Senate	House	Total U.S.
Percent who are women	16	17	51
Percent who are African American	1	10	13
Percent who are Hispanic	3	6	13
Percent who are Asian	2	<1	4

(Senate and House source: Wikepedia; total U.S. source: U.S. Census. These numbers are very close, but not identical to another data source, GMCL.org.)

As you can see, while the political class expects the rest of us to adhere to defined affirmative action law and policy, they continue to be heavily skewed to white males. If a private company followed their behavior there would likely be ramifications, but the political class obviously believes they are above the laws they pass for the rest of America. Thus, this change would force them to either become more balanced in their representation of America or suffer the same penalties the rest of us do.

Let them eat cake: just another sad example of having both parties tell us what to do while they do as they please.

What do Washington's politicians and pro wrestlers have in common? … They're mostly overweight white guys pretending to hurt each other.

—author unknown

Step 46

Subject all government agencies, including
Congress, to a strict auditing process, similar to
Sarbanes-Oxley procedures, to ensure prudent use
and tracking of taxpayer assets and funds.

Quick, name the biggest employer, purchasing entity, and consumption entity in the country. It is not General Electric, it is not Walmart, and it is not General Motors. The United States government has more employees and buys and consumes more services and products than any entity in the whole country. However, while U.S. corporations have to adhere to overly strict and repressive accounting analysis and reporting requirements as outlined by the Sarbanes-Oxley Act, the U.S. government is under no such mandate. As a result, billions of dollars in hard-earned taxpayer money is lost every year to lax accounting standards (see the Department of Agriculture example cited previously).

Despite controlling the most wealth in the country, the political class and the government it runs has not seen fit to get it under control from an accounting perspective and, more importantly, an accountability perspective. Thus, what is good for us should be good for the government. Federal department heads and the chairpersons of the responsible congressional committees should be subject to the same strict reporting and accountability laws, such as Sarbanes-Oxley, that the rest of the country has to abide by.

Failure to properly account for taxpayer funds could result in a full spectrum of results, up to and including prison time, and would apply both to the bureaucrats running the federal departments and the congressional people responsible for overseeing them. Tightening up the accounting in the federal government would probably free up billions of dollars in missing funds and also give Congress an idea of what types of anxiety their programs usually produce.

This accountability would help tame the Jabba the Hutt characteristic of current-day U.S. government, providing accountability for the voracious and wasteful use of taxpayer dollars.

You don't pay taxes—they take taxes."

—*Chris Rock*

Step 47

Force the federal wing of the political class to get out of two major areas of national interest where they have constantly misspent taxpayer money, returning the responsibility back to the states: farm subsidies and highways.

Nowhere has the political class screwed up markets or wasted more taxpayer money than in the areas of farm subsidies and highway construction. A recent farm subsidy bill exceeding $300 billion in costs was passed by Congress (*The Week* magazine, May 30, 2008). Despite record-high farm prices, the political class continues to bribe farmers (with your taxpayer money) and others for their votes and continues to extend corporate welfare to farming businesses. Plus, the bill also contains wasteful programs such as a tax break for racehorse owners. This wasteful spending bill costs each American household about $2,400. Tens of billions of dollars have also been wasted by the government on transportation programs. And what have these subsidies done for America:

- A high percentage of farm subsidies have gone to the mega/corporate growers and not the family farms, resulting in a farm industry corporate welfare program that enhances private company shareholder value at the expense of the ordinary taxpayer.

- Farm subsidies "generally encourage inefficient farmers to grow unprofitable crops far beyond what consumers need, secure in the knowledge that the government will help protect them from loss" (as quoted in the *St. Petersburg Times* on August 22, 2007, reprinted from the *New York Times*).

- To further illustrate the absurdity of letting the political class administer a farm subsidy program, consider the following facts from *Reason* magazine (December, 2007) under the article "Green Acres."

  Between 2003 and 2005, hundreds of New York city residents, most of whom lived in Manhattan, that great farming mecca of the northeast, received farm subsidy payments of $4.2 million.

  Two of these "struggling agrarians" in New York City included Mark Rockefeller and David Rockefeller.

  Between 2003 and 2005, $9.4 billion in taxpayer-funded crop subsidies went to individuals who claimed them through "partnerships, joint ventures, corporations, or other business entities." That is, billions of dollars were handed out to people who never set foot on a farm.

- Federal highway programs have not only wasted taxpayer money (the "bridge to nowhere" in Alaska would have spent hundreds of millions of dollars to link up a small remote Alaskan tribe to the mainland), but have also killed Americans. The Federal Big Dig project in Boston not only exceeded budget by more than sevenfold, but also killed Milena DelValle when a ceiling tile dropped onto her car. In Minnesota, a bridge on Interstate 35W collapsed, killing thirteen Americans.

Given that the federal wing of the political class has bungled badly in both of these areas, it is time for them to get out of them. This step would likely result in far less pork barrel programs, helping to reduce taxes and wasted money, and would return control to the states where there would be more local accountability and control, and hopefully better control.

This withdrawal would be accomplished in the following manner:

- Farm subsidies for the family farm would be phased out over a five-year period, giving them time to adjust to a competitive marketplace.

- Farm subsidies to all mega-farms and corporations would be phased out immediately, causing the shareholders to assume the financial burden of running the companies, not the taxpayers.

- The federal highway tax on gasoline would be reduced 90 percent over a three-year period. This would allow existing federal programs to be finished out while removing the pot of money that the political class has abused for so long to be reduced to 10 percent of what it is today. That 10 percent would be used only to help facilitate transportation projects across state lines; it would never be used for an intrastate transportation project.

- If the states want to do their own transportation projects, they could increase their state tax on gasoline to fill the void left when federal transportation money dried out, replacing all or some of the tax on gasoline at the federal level that was removed. This step would guarantee that taxpayers in the other forty-nine states would not subsidize pork highway projects in one state, as for the Alaskan bridge to nowhere.

The political class would howl if these two changes ever came up for a vote. These changes would remove a substantial amount of power that the political class has grabbed and abused over the years. However, most economists would agree that farm subsidies are inefficient and result in higher prices for all of us. The *St. Petersburg Times* article quoted above laid out how the removal of farm subsidies in New Zealand in 1984 led to a booming farm industry in New Zealand: "Today, agriculture remains the lifeblood of New Zealand's economy. There are more sheep and cows here than people, their meat, milk, and wool providing the country with its biggest source of export earnings. Most farms are owned by families, but their incomes have recovered and output has soared."

For transportation, the state level of the political class cannot do a worse job at managing the country's highways than the federal branch, so why not try it? The states could not print money or steal money from other states when a transportation project goes over budget (e.g., the Big Dig in Boston, originally budgeted for about $2 billion but exceeding $14 billion), so, hopefully, state oversight of highway projects would be done more efficiently. Also, the states are much closer to the their highway users from a voting perspective, and if ceiling tiles and collapsed bridges start killing their citizens, they are more likely to feel the heat at election time than some federal bureaucrat.

The final reason for removing the federal political class from these two areas is to return control back to individual citizens by reducing waste and taxes, and pushing responsibility to a more local level, closer to the American citizen.

This is a classic useless used car situation, with the federal wing of the political class wasting billions of taxpayer dollars on inefficient farm subsidies and wasteful and fatal highway programs.

Politicians are the same all over. They will build you a bridge even when there is no river.

—*Nikita Khrushev*

Corporate
Governance

Step 48

Repeal the Sarbanes-Oxley law for America businesses immediately. The vast majority of companies in this country have never been found guilty of corporate and accounting malfeasance, and those who have been accused have been convicted.

During the 1990s, under the Clinton administration's SEC, a number of companies (Enron, Worldcom, Aegis, Qwest, and others) became lax in their accounting and auditing practices, resulting in obscene windfall monetary compensation for high-ranking executives within those companies. Not only were the practices lax, but they were usually also unlawful. Unfortunately, it was not until the Bush administration were these lawbreakers brought to justice. By then, the pensions and savings plans of thousands of people, both inside and outside those companies breaking the law, were ruined.

As a result of these actions, the political class put into effect the Sarbanes-Oxley Act, requiring just about every public company in the country to do an incredible amount of overkill work to justify the accuracy of their accounting methods and output, and having the executives of those companies sign off on the validity of their results. This requires every company to devote a significant amount of accounting, legal, and other resources to comply with the law even though they themselves have never run afoul of generally accepted accounting practices and SEC disclosure requirements.

The fallacy of this law is that no one in the government actually reviews this mountain of accounting work unless there is a problem in the future. The work of all of these resources is usually completed and then condemned to never be seen again, defeating the whole purpose of the act, which was to catch corporate accounting fraud schemes. Remember, not every company in America was cheating on their accounting practices in the 1990s. Of the almost seventeen thousand public companies in the U.S. (Source: crmz. org, Credit Risk Monitor), apparently only a handful were up to no good. The vast majority were doing their due diligence and trying to put forth the best accounting numbers available. However, since the SEC/government/political class were not on the job in the 1990s, every American company has to suffer under these onerous Sarbanes-Oxley guidelines.

Wasting resources on another government failure such as Sarbanes-Oxley puts American industries under another competitive disadvantage in the global marketplace. Might these accounting and legal resources be better spent on competing with the Chinese and Indian corporations and not creating work that will likely never see the light of day? Besides wasting resources, the act has caused a number of companies to go private and remove themselves from the burdens of the law. Companies should go private because it is the best thing to do in the marketplace, not because the political class wants to look like they are doing something constructive.

Thus, the act should be repealed at once, and the SEC should start doing its job, which it has not done since the scandals from the 1990s broke. The best deterrent to corporate misbehavior is to strengthen the SEC, increase the white-collar penalties for white-collar crime, and require any company convicted of corporate accounting lawbreaking to go forward under the Sarbanes-Oxley requirements.

These three things would help keep the corporate lawbreakers in line, free up resources for global competition, and reinforce the American tradition of being innocent until proven guilty. Under Sarbanes-Oxley you are assumed to be guilty and must prove that you are not by developing and filing an obscene amount of unread analysis and work.

This five-legged-dog program does not protect investors from bad accounting like it claims to do; it only wastes valuable American corporate resources. By freeing innocent companies from doing this onerous work, American competitiveness would increase, as resources wasted on compliance would be redirected to improving the economic health of the country and freeing American corporations from the prying eyes of the political class.

> **A wise and frugal government, which shall leave men free to regulate their own pursuits of industry and improvement, and shall not take from the mouth of labor and bread it has earned—this is the sum of good government."**
>
> *— Thomas Jefferson*

Step 49

Do not permit executive and individual employee compensation (including salary, bonus, options, and the value of other non-monetary perks) exceeding $3,000,000 a year to be tax deductible as a business expense.

Consider the statistics cited in an August 29, 2007, article at cnnmoney.com:

- In 2006 the average CEO of a large U.S. company made roughly $10.6 million or 364 times that of U.S. full-time and part-time workers, according to a joint analysis released by the liberal Institute for Policy Studies and United for a Fair Economy.

- If you consider the average compensation (wages plus benefits) for only full-time, year-round workers in nonmanagerial jobs, roughly $40,000, CEO pay is 270 times larger.

- This is up almost fourfold from 71 times that of the average worker in 1989.

Government should never be in the business of regulating and managing compensation in the private sector of the country. First, given their incompetence in everything else, they will never be able to do it correctly, efficiently, or in a timely manner. Second, in a free country the market should set prices, costs, salaries, etc., in order to allow resources to flow the most efficiently.

However, given this, it does make sense for some action to be taken to better level the playing field when it comes to executive compensation. Since salary (and other forms of compensation) is a tax-deductible expense when a corporation fills out its income taxes, every taxpayer in the country subsidizes these big salaries and compensation levels. Remember, government does not create wealth, it only takes wealth from its citizens, and the less wealth it takes from others, the more wealth must be taken from everyone else.

This change accomplishes a number of objectives. It does not allow the political class/government to set executive compensation levels in private industry. However, it does cap the amount of tax benefits those corporations can achieve by exceeding the $3 million guideline. Companies can pay anything they want, but the extraordinary pay levels will not be borne by the American taxpayer. If the executives are paid more than $3 million, then the tax burden on the company, not the taxpayer, gets steeper.

The $3 million cap on tax deductibility is easily calculated by multiplying the $40 thousand average total compensation of the average full-time worker by the 71 times multiplier for CEO pay in 1989. This yields a figure of $2,840,000 which is rounded to $3 million.

Please note that the change proposed relates to any employee of the firm, not just the top executive. This change would have ramifications for many fields, including professional sports. Teams would still be able to pay their top stars any amount they desired, but the American taxpayer would no longer be the bearer of some of the more outlandish salaries that exist in the pro sports. Thus, if the New York Yankees want to pay Alex Rodriguez $25 million a year, they can go right ahead and do so. However, the entire $25 million would not be tax deductible by the team; only the first $3 million could be taken as a business tax deduction.

Remember, the $3 million cap is on total compensation, not just straight salaries/wages. Stock options, private use of company airplanes and facilities, special monetary grants, etc., would be used in the tax cap calculation.

This is a freedom pyramid issue in that ordinary American citizens indirectly subsidize outsized corporate compensation levels through the tax deductibility of these compensation levels. By capping the tax friendliness of these compensation levels, the tax burden on most citizens should be lessened.

We do not have a money problem in America. We have a values and priorities problem.

—Marian Wright Edelman

What You Can Do

Step 50

Go to our website on a regular basis:
www.loathemygovernment.com.

There are several activities that require your participation to help make these fifty changes a reality:

- We have posted these changes for online review and reading. Every two years we will be polling members of Congress on these proposed changes to our country's affairs and posting their answers on the website along with the constituents each member serves. Also posted will be a composite score to quickly indicate where your representatives fall relative to freedom. Those who do not respond to the survey will be graded out as zero.

- In another website section, we will be posting specific spending programs and projects that are either before Congress or that have recently passed. You can vote online to say whether or not you think these programs are a good value for your federal tax dollar. We believe that most of them are not worthy of our tax dollars (remember the federally funded pet inventory project for that California county mentioned previously), but you can tell us how you feel by voting. Results will be sent to current political class politicians on a regular basis.

- The real power of the website, however, is in its action committees. Each of the proposed changes of this book will have an online action committee of volunteers whose job is to see that these changes are implemented by the political class. Each committee will be a self-contained effort, but it can obviously have citizens who are members of more than one committee and can share helpful information across committees. Each committee will organize itself as it sees fit once enough volunteers have signed up to reach critical mass. They will set up their own governance structure and action program. Members can include both individuals or existing organizations that want to join in.

By dividing up the needed changes into smaller groups, constant, focused pressure can be brought to bear on the political class. This also allows more people to be actively involved by not having a small group try to do everything, but spreading the workload and responsibility across the nation.

- The fourth section of the website will be a place where people can suggest cost savings, identify waste and fraud, point out misinformation in the press, and suggest tactics to use to move these changes forward. These postings will be forwarded to the relevant action committees for review and action.

If you go to one demonstration and then go home, that's something, but the people in power can live with that. What they can't live with is sustained pressure that keeps building, organizations that keep doing things, people that keep learning lessons from the last time and doing it better the next time.

—*Noam Chomsky*

The Ultimate Step!

Act like you love freedom and respect the rights of others to do the same.

Implementing these changes will be very difficult. The political class is entrenched and will not give up their power over you easily and willingly. However, nothing will be accomplished unless Americans in all walks of life start cherishing freedom themselves and respecting the rights of other Americans to have the same freedoms they want. This requires any number of actions including, but not limited, to the following:

- Do not run to your current politician to act when you want something at the expense of another American. Chances are you will not get what you want, and whatever actions are taken as a result of your request will not likely increase the level of freedom in this country. Don't like gay Americans? Fine. Just don't hang out with them; do not ask a wing of the political class you favor to act against them. Don't like the rich? Fine, but realize the majority of the rich in this country got that way the old-fashioned way: by working hard and saving. Don't ask the political class to punish them for those noble traits. Remember, the rich pay the vast majority of taxes in this country.

- In fact, do not ask the political class to do anything for you if you can help it. It only empowers them more at the expense of everyone's freedom.

As mentioned previously, the political class wins when they divide Americans into "tribes" and let the tribes fight each other when the main culprit in our country's decline is the politicians themselves. By keeping us occupied with each other, they continue to rule and plunder both our wallets and our freedoms.

- Do not fall into the old trap that says, "He may be a bastard, but he's our bastard" Just because a member of the political class has been reelected many times does not mean he or she is good for America. Many surveys of voter satisfaction show that voters are not happy with Congress but believe their own representatives are okay. They may think their representatives are good because they got some specific pork barrel spending to become a reality. The reason for reelection should be because a candidate is good for both the sending district/state *and* the country as a whole.

  Thus, in the future, make a special effort to see if the member of the political class you are faced with serves both constituencies, the local area and the country. If not, vote them out of office for someone who will. Remember, their first priority is reelection and the consolidation of power, not the betterment of the country. When in doubt, vote against all incumbents because the non-incumbents probably cannot do a worse job. At least with the non-incumbents you have a chance at meaningful change. Given the current situation in the country, what have we got to lose by dumping the members of the political class that got us into the mess we are in now?

- Apply the changes discussed in this book and compare them to issues that the political class faces and how they act on them. Did they act in the country's best interests or in the interest of their own need for power? Did they act to further the rights and wishes of one American tribe over another? Did they act morally relative to a noble set of shared values and behaviors? Soon you will see how most of their actions are not in the best interests of the country. Beware the five-legged dog!

- With regards to media, look for different and varied ways of getting your news. Understand that most major news out-looks today are not unbiased, and each has its own political slant and favorite wing of the ruling political class. If you do not diversify your information sources, you will continue to be fed the same messages that the political class wants you to hear, messages that divert your attention from the real needs of the country, and allow the political class to proceed with their freedom and power grab. Without actively looking for different ways to get your information, you will be forced to live with the message that the political class wants you to hear as forced through the media outlets they want you to use. You will become a warrior in their tribal fight against other Americans. Fortunately, the Internet makes the search for alternative sources quite easy and frees you to get a var-ied set of information sources to act upon.

- Be passionate but not emotional. Passionate people firmly and calmly believe in what they are doing and have logic, data, information, and understanding to support their po-sition, making them a very formidable force. They are not likely to fall into the tribal warfare trap that the political class will rely on. Emotional people do not have a foundation to resist the ploys and lies of the political class, usually lacking an understanding of the root cause of the country's problems and their own problems.

The death of democracy is not likely to be an assassination from ambush. It will be a slow extinction from apathy, indifference, and undernourishment.

—*Robert M. Hutchins*

Closing Thoughts

I f you learned anything from reading this book it is that the government, as operated by the single existing political class in this country, is not looking out for your welfare, your wealth, your safety, or the best interests of the country. They are looking out for their wealth, their egos, themselves, and the best interests of the government, which they run and control.

This country was not created and defended many times to have the type of elitist ruling class that exists today. It was created to allow individuals to freely go about their lives as they see fit, using their brains, effort, and wealth to do what they want, when they want, and for whom they want as long as it does not interfere with others doing the same thing. The creation and acceptance of the concept of "the common good" at the expense of individual freedom, with the definition of the common good defined by the political class as it sees fit, is the biggest danger to this country today. It robs people of their wealth and freedom, stifles innovation, and sets one group of Americans against another.

Michael Douglas, in his role as the president of the United States in the movie *The American President*, summarized it best when he described how the political class works (Bob Rumson is his main political rival in the film): "And whatever your particular problem is, I promise you Bob Rumson is not the least bit interested in solving it. He is interested in two things, and two things only: making you afraid of it, and telling you who's to blame for it. That, ladies and gentlemen, is how you win elections."

Politically, this is where we, as a nation, are today. However, there is hope for change if you examine the following excerpt from the Declaration of Independence:

> That whenever any Form of Government becomes destructive of the ends, it is the right of the People to alter or to abolish it, and to institute new Government, laying its foundation on such principles and organizing its power it such form, as to them shall seem most likely to effect their Safety and Happiness. Prudence, indeed, will dictate that Governments long established should not be changed for light and transient causes; and accordingly all experience hath shown that mankind are more disposed to suffer, while evils are sufferable than to right themselves by abolishing the forms to which they are accustomed. But when a long train of abuses and usurpations, pursuing invariably the same Object evinces a design to reduce them under absolute Despotism, it is their right, it is their duty, to throw off such Government, and to provide new Guards for their future security.

Hopefully, this book has identified the problem: the current political class. The above paragraph should be the call to action. We need to take its advice and restore the ideals that made this country great. Remember, no matter how audacious hope is, hope is not a strategy. These first fifty steps can be that strategy to fix what the political class has broken.

The hottest place in hell is reserved for those that remain neutral during times of moral crisis.

—Dante

Appendices

Appendix A

More Political Class Insanity—Part One

Consider the following information that was published in *Parade Magazine's* Intelligence Report on November 6, 2005 and January 27, 2008, which highlighted what some of your federal tax dollars are being spent on:

- $250,000 for research to cut asparagus industry labor costs.

- $200,000 to Ocean Spray to market white cranberry juice in Great Britain.

- $2,000,000 to construct a parking facility at the University of Incarnate World, a Catholic institution in San Antonio, despite adequate existing parking facilities.

- $70,000 for a Paper Industry Hall of Fame in Wisconsin.

- $26,000,000 to operate the Selective Service, even though there has not been any military draft since 1973.

- $519,000,000 in farm subsidies, between 1995 and 2003, to Riceland Foods in Arkansas. Riceland receives more federal money in a typical year than all the farmers in twelve other states combined.

- $300,000 for a feasibility study for the world's first fully enclosed motor speedway in Ohio.

- $150,000 to the Grammy Foundation to support Grammy Camp, where sixty students learn the music business.

- $775,000 to the Biltmore Hotel in Coral Gables, Florida—part of a project to provide economic opportunity in areas of low or moderate income. However, Coral Gables' per capita income is almost 20 percent above the national average.

- $213,000 for olive fruit fly research in France.

- $1,900,000 for the Center for Grape Genetics in New York.

- $2,500,000 for fish waste research in Alaska.

- $1,200,000 for cormorant control in several states (cormorants are birds - this is one example where you honestly say your taxpayer money is "for the birds", "flying the coop", etc.).

Unfortunately, this is just a very, very small sample of the waste the political class foists on the American taxpayer every year. Even so, the above items total out to about $554,000,000. According to calculations contained in another *Parade* Intelligence Report article published July 1, 2007, this $554,000,000 could also have been spent on the following:

- Treatment and prevention of about 83,000,000 cases of malaria in Africa.

- Basic health insurance for about 137,000 Americans.

- About 230,000,000 school lunches for needy children in America.

- 3,700 new, fully armored Humvees for U.S. troops in Iraq and elsewhere.

There has to be a better way to serve America than what the political class is doing to us now.

Appendix B

More Political Class Insanity—Part 2

onsider some recent public examples and consider this: are these the people you want leading this country and spending your tax dollars?

The *St. Petersburg Times* printed a story from wire service reports on January 19, 2008 concerning the major crisis unfolding in the banking industry relating to subprime mortgages. Specifically, it highlighted a meeting held by the House Budget Committee which was hearing testimony from Federal Reserve Chairman Ben Bernanke and attended by Representative Marcy Kaptur, D-Ohio. Unfortunately, it appears Ms. Kaptur did not come prepared to the meeting since she had difficulty understanding who Mr. Bernanke was. She confused him with Treasury Secretary Henry Paulson, asking numerous questions in trying to understand the backgrounds, work histories and responsibilities of Mr. Bernanke and Mr. Paulson. Mr. Bernanke had to lay out the difference between the two before the meeting could go on.

Comment: With the nation in the midst of a colossal financial crisis, a member of the political class, sitting on an important congressional committee, did not take the time or have the smarts to understand who the major players are in government relative to the crisis. Is it any wonder we are in the subprime mortgage mess we are in when the people in charge are so ignorant of the situation?

Published in the *St. Petersburg Times* from the Associated Press on December 21, 2007 (excerpts below):

- The IRS paid a contractor $188,000 to provide one person to do clerical work over 11 months—work that has been done by a government employee of ranking GS-7 for a starting salary of about $38,000 plus benefits.

- The Treasury Department's inspector general for tax administration said the IRS needlessly spent almost $2,000,000 on a computer security system the tax agency does not plan using at this time.

- The inspector general also found that the IRS did not maintain documents to back up costs, saying it was only able to account for about 70 percent of the spending.

Comment: this is your tax money being misspent, a scenario that is likely being repeated thousands of times every day with the political class doing nothing to stop it.

An article published in the sports section of the *St. Petersburg Times* on June 13, 2007 reported that Scottie Pippen, a famous and rich National Basketball Association all star player, earned over $78,000 in Federal government checks for land he owns in Arkansas, according to CNBC. Nowhere in the article did it say the government bought the land, it said he earned the money from the government. This payment was made to him despite the fact that he has earned over $100,000,000 in his NBA career. The article also pointed out that he had lost a lot of it through bad investments.

Comment: Glad we could use taxpayer money to help Scottie get through his difficult time. It's not easy living on the tens of millions of dollars he probably still has left.

The *St. Petersburg Times* printed an article from the Associated Press on October 3, 2007 (excerpts below):

In a one year period, Federal employees wasted over $140,000,000 on business- or first-class airline tickets, breaking the rules in some cases simply because they felt entitled according to congressional investigators.

A political appointee at the Pentagon took fifteen premium-class flights and cited a medical condition as justification. However, the only evidence was a note signed by a fellow Pentagon employee, not a physician.

Comment: this is what they found; the number is probably higher.

Published in *Reason Magazine*, December, 2007:

But even with those new disclosure requirements, earmarks are as popular as ever with 6,500 earmarks totaling almost $11 billion in this cycle. Apparently every congressman knows exactly how much his colleagues have managed to score for their home districts, that just makes the competition fiercer … This season's more egregious earmarks include $100,000 for a prison museum in Kansas and $250,000 for a "wine and culinary center" in Washington state.

Comment: While wasting money for projects such as these and hundreds of others like them is bad enough, think about the time that is wasted scrambling for funding. This is time that your elected representatives are not spending on reducing the deficit, getting out of foreign entanglements, solving the health care crisis, etc., etc., etc.

Published in *Reason Magazine*, December, 2007:

The decades-old benefit concert called Farm Aid came to New York City for the first time ever in September. And fittingly so: Willie Nelson's crusade to save the family farm has never been so relevant to Park Avenue. In the map below [not included], the red dots represent Manhattan residents raking in federal agricultural subsidies. The larger dots represent those collecting the largest payments, including such struggling agrarians as Mark and David Rockefeller.

The Environmental Working Group, a nonprofit organization that works to reduce environmentally harmful subsidies, estimates that between 2003 and 2005, $9.4 billion in taxpayer-funded crop subsidies went to individuals who claimed them through "partnerships, joint ventures, corporations, or other business entities." Payments to New York City residents totaled $4.2 million during the same period. That's a tiny slice of the subsidy pie, but it's indicative of the level of waste and fraud in the system.

Comment: maybe Scotty Pippen should move his farming operation to New York City to increase his take in the subsidy pie.

Other wasteful political class spending, published in *The Week Magazine*, April 25, 2008 (excerpts):

- $500,000 for a "Teapot Museum" in North Carolina

- $3,000,000 to the First Tee Organization, whose mission is to "promote character development and life-enhancing values through the game of golf"

- $500,000 to buy twenty-one train cabooses to be repurposed for a "caboose motel" in Titusville, Pennsylvania

- $150,000 for fixing plumbing in Bronx, New York, Italian restaurants

- $300,000 for San Francisco's Exploratorium Science Museum

Comment: it never ends—the waste of resources, time, and money—all so a select few people can get elected over and over again.

According to a recent Rasmussen poll, as reported in *The Week Magazine* in its October 17, 2008 edition, 59 percent of Americans say they would vote to replace the entire United States Congress rather than vote to keep it intact. Only 23 percent of the respondents say they have any confidence that Congress has the ability to fix the current economic problems facing the country.

Comment: perhaps the country is finally realizing that the current members of the political class are incapable or unwilling to make the difficult and complicated decisions necessary to get the country back on track.

Reported on Earthlink on April 6, 2008, under the news title "GAO: Millions Wasted On Gov't Cards" (excerpts):

- An Agriculture Department employee wrote 180 convenience checks for more than $642,00 to a live-in boyfriend over a six-year period. The money was used for gambling, car and mortgage payments, dinners, and retail purchases that went unnoticed until USDA's inspector general received a tip from a whistle-blower.

- U.S. postal workers separately billed more than $14,000 to government credit cards for Internet dating services and a dinner at Ruth Chris Steakhouse in Orlando, Florida, for eighty-one people at a cost of $160 each for steak and crabs.

- At the Pentagon, four employees purchased $77,700 in clothing and accessories at high-end clothing and sporting goods stores. The spending included more than $45,000 at Brooks Brothers and similar stores for tailor-made suits.

- At the State Department, one credit card holder bought $360 worth of women's lingerie at Seduction Boutique for use during jungle training by trainees of a drug enforcement program in Ecuador.

Comment: while these are atrocious wastes of taxpayer money, imagine how much more waste goes on with government-issued credit cards that has not been uncovered.

In the August 3, 2008, issue of *Parade Magazine*, Sharon Male reported that the current edition of Congress, the 110th, had passed less legislation than any Congress in the last tens years, just 260 laws. More distressing, of those 260 laws, seventy-four, or about 28 percent of them, had to do with renaming post offices. This Congress also passed numerous resolutions, including:

- One resolution that recognized soil as an essential resource.

- Another resolution congratulating the UC-Irvine volleyball team.

- A third resolution recognizing June 30 as National Corvette Day.

Ms. Male quotes Representative John Shimkus (R., Ill.) who said: "It's probably not the best use of our time, but we have to do something. These resolutions make it look like we're working."

Comment: I think Representative Shimkus's comment says it all.

On October 4, 2008, the *St. Petersburg Times* reported that the $800,000,000,000 financial bailout bill that was rushed through Congress included provisions to provide a tax break to manufacturers of wooden arrows for children, provided the ability of NASCAR to write off racetrack costs over seven years, and provided a rebate against excise taxes charged on imported rum from Puerto Rico and the Virgin Islands.

Comment: in the midst of the greatest financial crisis facing the the country since the Great Depression, the political class still has the time, the energy, and the nerve to worry about petty, trivial issues regarding arrows, NASCAR, and imported rum.

On September 24, 2008, the *St. Petersburg Times* reported that the government, through the Medicare program, paid more than $1,000,000,000 in claims for such questionable uses as blood glucose strips for sexual impotence according to congressional investigators. They found that billions of dollars may have been spent through the years because Medicare paid out claims with blank or invalid diagnosis codes.

Comment: most politicians, in order to get elected, are promising sweeping health coverage even though current government health programs waste billions of taxpayer dollars with just the programs and responsibilities they have today.

In early December, 2008, Senate Majority Leader Henry Reid was widely quoted as stating, "In the summertime … you could literally smell the tourists coming into the Capital."

Comment: It is one thing to think your fellow citizens smell; it is another thing to state it out loud at a public gathering. It illustrates the elitist attitude and contempt the political class holds for the typical American citizen.

On January 4, 2009, the *St. Petersburg Times* ran a *New York Times* article that outlined how Senator Hillary Clinton helped get millions of dollars of assistance for a mall development project around the same time the owner of that project donated $100,000 to Bill Clinton's foundation. The legislation allowed the use of tax-free bonds to finance the mall's construction, and another $5 million was placed into a highway bill for roadway construction around the mall.

Comment: The political class shows no shame at all. Even if there was no quid pro quo, the appearance of conflict of interest is just as bad as an actual conflict of interest. It undermines the integrity of the entire political system. No part of the government should serve as a personal bank account for the political class.

On December 10, 2008, the lead article on the front page of the *St. Petersburg Times* reported how the sitting governor of Illinois, Rod Blagojevich, was being charged by federal prosecutors for illegally trying to sell the appointment to fill Barak Obama's vacant Senate seat to the highest bidder. According to the report, Blagojevich was alleged to have said in an FBI wiretrap: "I'm going to keep this Senate option for me a real possibility, you know, and therefore I can drive a hard bargain. You hear what I'm saying. And if I don't get what I want and I'm not satisfied with it, then I'll just take the seat myself … is a (expletive) valuable thing, you just don't give it away for nothing."

Comment: I think the governor said it all.

On November 26, 2008, the *News Journal* in Wilmington, Delaware, summarized the federal government's spending efforts to rescue the economy. These efforts included loans to banks and money market funds, the backing of Fannie Mae and Freddie Mac assets, buying up the bad debt from financial institutions, and the purchasing of mortgage-backed assets. If you add up all of the costs and potential liabilities the political class has incurred to fix an economic disaster that was largely their own doing and include the $800 billion stimulus package that was passed in early 2009, the total comes to about $6.5 trillion. Since there are about 130 million United States households, every household is now on the hook for about $50,000.

Comment: Rather than give the big banks and brokerage houses the money, would it not have been better to give every household a $50,000 check? This approach would have eliminated the foreclosure problem, probably kick-started the automobile industry's sales, spurred overall consumer spending, and possibly ended the financial crisis in short order. Some banks would have gone out of business because of the bad loans they made and bad debt they incurred, but so what? They deserve to die given their greed and lack of financial discipline. With $6.5 trillion injected directly into the economy, new banks and financial institutions would have arisen to serve the market need. The $6.5 trillion is the American taxpayer's responsibility to repay; should not the average American gotten a substantial share of it?

On December 11, 2008, the *St. Petersburg Times* ran an AP story describing how many of the financial institutions receiving federal bailout help were also big contributors to the Democratic and Republican national conventions. AIG, Citigroup, Goldman Sachs, and Freddie Mac (a government entity!) donated $3.1 million to the conventions.

Comment: Maybe that is why the average American citizen was not getting any of the $6.5 trillion. We did not help the Democrats and Republicans to party at their conventions, and they decided to cut us out of the financial rescue process.

Appendix C

More Political Class Insanity—Part 3

Want to get in on the fun? Use the following chart to track and document any type of political class insanity, and then upload your findings to our website to be shared with other freedom-loving Americans.

Date of the insanity	Political class members causing the insanity	Documented source of the insanity	Describe the insanity

Appendix D

The original intention for Appendix D was to reprint an article that appeared in US News and World Report in May, 2006. The article was written by Dan Gilgoff and was titled: "A Fake Democracy? Why no one has much chance of toppling Congress's incumbents." Mr. Gilgoff elegantly laid out how the political class has rigged the election process through Congressional district gerrymandering and control of campaign funds and resources to virtually ensure that current politicians will almost always be able to keep their Congressional seats for as long as they want them. However, *US News and World Report* would not grant reprint permission so the article is not reprinted here. We would suggest that interested readers go to their website archives to find Mr. Gilgoff's article; it highlights many of the issues addressed in this book.

Appendix E

The Fallacy of Social Security As a Wise Retirement Investment

Politicians are always using the Social Security system as a tool to pit one American tribe against another, the result being that nothing ever changes and the system hurtles toward insolvency. One of the most emotional arguments is that the current system is safer and better than private investment. To test this theory, I analyzed my own relationships with the Social Security system to theoretically see if my Social Security deductions would have been better off if I had kept the funds myself rather than trusting the political class to manage my retirement contributions.

The assumptions in my analysis were as follows:

- Starting in 1969, the first year I contributed to the system, I would have been able to keep both my contributions and my employer's contributions on my behalf to the Social Security system.

- All of the contributions would have been totally invested in an S&P 500 stock index fund that mimicked the S&P 500 index.

- Dividends were not reinvested in order to estimate a more conservative return.

- In 2008 and beyond, I converted all of the accumulated funds to a very conservative bond fund that generated a safe, but conservative, 4 percent annual return on average.

- The Social Security Administration told me that if I started to withdraw from the system at age sixty-two, I would receive $1,357 per month.

- However, under the above assumption set, I could begin withdrawing $4,200 a month at age sixty-two from my accumulated savings and investments until I was over a hundred years old. In other words, I would have been able to receive *three times* the amount every month during retirement if I had been allowed to invest my contributions myself in the stock market until I was over a hundred years old.

In 1998, The Heritage Foundation came up with similar results. According to the analysis on their website, the average married couple in an average income household could expect to receive about $450,000 worth of Social Security benefits in their lifetime (1997 dollars). If they had been able to take their personal and their employer's contributions and invested them half in T-bills and half in equities, they would have amassed about $975,000 (1997 dollars) for retirement, more than twice the amount they will receive from Social Security.

The Social Security system is not a good deal for anyone but the political class. It allows them to perpetuate lies about the viability of private investment, energize their bases to repel any changes to the system, pit one tribe against another (e.g., rich versus poor, old versus young), and maintain another form of control over the citizens of this country, resulting in lost freedom of choice for us all.

It's time to join a citizen-based action plan.
Help implement the fifty first steps at the grassroots level.

www.LoatheMyGovernment.com

Through this website, individual Americans can sign up for any of
the fifty action committees and become part of the solution.